W9-DFP-283

Re-Thinking the Network Economy

Re-Thinking the Network Economy

The True Forces That Drive the Digital Marketplace

STAN J. LIEBOWITZ

AMACOM

American Management Association

New York • Atlanta • Brussels • Buenos Aires • Chicago • Mexico City
San Francisco • Shanghai • Tokyo • Toronto • Washington, D.C.

This publication is designed to provide accurate and authoritative information in regard to the subject matter covered. It is sold with the understanding that the publisher is not engaged in rendering legal, accounting, or other professional service. If legal advice or other expert assistance is required, the services of a competent professional person should be sought.

Library of Congress Cataloging-in-Publication Data

Liebowitz, S. J., 1950–
    Re-thinking the network economy: the true forces that drive the digital marketplace / Stan J. Liebowitz.
        p. cm.
   Includes index.
   ISBN 0-8144-0649-1
    1. Electronic commerce.   2. Internet.   I. Title: True forces that drive the digital marketplace.   II. Title.

HF5548.32 .L534   2002
381'.1—dc21

2002006196

Printing number

10 9 8 7 6 5 4 3 2 1

Contents

Preface

In the Fall of 1995, Netscape had recently had its IPO, and I watched its shares soar. I considered its price to be wildly unrealistic and quickly shorted it. I wasn't sure what business model Netscape was going to apply to make the type of profits that would justify its seemingly lofty market capitalization. After a few ups and downs, I was able to make a small profit, but Netscape's fortunes were thwarted more by Microsoft's introduction of Internet Explorer than by any realism that had returned to the market.

After Netscape, I shorted Yahoo in April of 1996, an action I was soon to regret. Stocks related to the Internet, particularly Yahoo, climbed to increasingly dizzying heights. I was way too early on the short side, and I soon found myself shorting a company that was undergoing one of the great financial run-ups of all time. I soon found myself deep in the red. After watching a very large chunk of the money that I had put away for my daughters' college education evaporate before my eyes, and after many a sleepless night, I threw in the towel in April of 1998. I took my losses and vowed to expose what I saw as insanity in the business press that was helping to stoke what was by then, as it appeared to me, a mad Internet frenzy among investors of all kinds. That was when I first conceived the idea of writing this book, both as a salve to my wounded ego and to help promote some sanity in a market I saw as totally insane. Not necessarily the best of motivations, but not the worst either.

My academic research in several related areas of economics seems to make me a particularly good fit to discuss e-commerce and other aspects of the Internet. I had done research on network effects and lock-in, two concepts that seemed to largely underpin the thinking that I saw displayed among the many uncritical Internet mavens. I had also done research on television advertising and the impact of new technologies on copyright owners. Ever since owning an Atari 800 in the early 1980s, I had read computer magazines for fun, and I had been an avid fan of technology for a very long time. It was my experience in these areas that convinced me that the Internet phenomenon was just a temporary, unsustainable aberration.

But working on this book soon took a back seat to another project that came up. My academic work with Stephen Margolis was suddenly propelled into the mass of publicity surrounding the Microsoft antitrust case. We were the leading critics of the theory on which the government was relying to support its case. We had thought about writing a book about those theories, and the Microsoft case provided a golden opportunity that we took advantage of during 1998. That book, *Winners, Losers, & Microsoft,* was published during 1999, and a revised version was published in 2001.

This current book took shape in early 2000, just before the onset of the Internet meltdown. Books about the Internet were everywhere and, in general, weren't selling all that well. A fortuitous circumstance, however, allowed me to show the book outline to the folks at AMACOM publishing, who in the fall of 2000 asked me to proceed with writing the manuscript.

For various personal reasons, the book has taken longer to write than it should have. By the time I was at the keyboard seriously writing the book I realized that, at the very least, I had to change all the tenses in the outline from the future to the past.

E-commerce is viewed quite differently now than it was when I began writing this book. At that time, firms with any Internet association were still highly valued, and those laggards who appeared to be missing the "wave" were being compared to lumbering dinosaurs, sure to fail in the years ahead.

How quickly things have changed. The technology meltdown

that has seen the Nasdaq average fall from over 5000 to below 2000 began with the decline of the Internet stocks. I was hoping when I began writing this book to help in a small way to bring some rationality to the market. My goals have changed as events have unfolded. Now I am content merely to provide some understanding of these markets.

Although Internet stock prices are now far more sensible, I still do not believe that there is much understanding of why things went awry. The Internet does provide important business opportunities. The main point learned in the last few years seems to be that firms need to be able to demonstrate the capability of generating profits some time in the future if they are to carry lofty stock valuations. Why the Internet stocks were not able to do so and which market models can still work on the Internet are, in my opinion, not much better understood now than they were at the height of the frenzy. This book, therefore, still has an important role to play.

I was able to change the tense from future to past without much difficulty. But it was far more difficult to keep up with the rapidity of market changes related to Internet commerce. The lengthy chapter on the sale of music online and the impacts of copying on sites such as Napster, for example, has been revised every few weeks since I first wrote it, and I am sure events will have made much of what is currently there passé by the time this book is published. Nevertheless, the concepts propounded in that material will remain unaltered.

I want to extend my appreciation to the folks at AMACOM who let the deadlines pass with nary a complaint.

I need to thank my frequent coauthor Steve Margolis for much of the material in chapters two and three. He was kind enough not only to let me rework in this book material that was as much his as mine, but, instead of criticizing me for this rather selfish act, he actually agreed to read through it. Of course, although he has coauthored many articles with me over the last decade, he is much better classified as a friend than a mere coauthor.

I also would like to thank my daughters, Tania and Lauren, who have heard about this book for several years and graciously acted as if they thought its publication was actually a worthwhile event.

I am grateful to the University of Texas–Dallas Management School and its dean, Hasan Pirkul, who helped support this research. My colleagues at UTD also listened to my complaints about writing a book that never seemed to be finished. Peter Lewin deserves special credit for having read through some of the manuscript.

Finally, over the last several years my students at UTD have used incomplete chapters as reading materials for my course in "The Economics of Information Goods." They made comments on several subject areas that improved the content.

A book like this, on a subject matter that changes so rapidly, is never really finished. News articles on these topics are coming out as I am sending the manuscript to the publisher. I hope that the main ideas in this book are more enduring than the particular facts to which they refer, which have evanescent lifespans.

Re-Thinking the Network Economy

Chapter 1

Introduction

The Internet changes everything. That was a common refrain just a very short time ago. Almost no one seems to believe it anymore.

In fact, the Internet changes very few of the tried-and-true business strategies. Like other important technological advances, the Internet will change many aspects of our lives. But the economic and business rules that worked in previous regimes will largely continue to work in the new regime. These rules of business endure because economic forces do not change—and cannot be changed by—mere changes in technology, no matter how much some of us might wish it were so. It is just our hubris at work when we start to think that our technology can change forces that are not of our conscious creation.

After reading this paragraph, the reader may ask: So why continue with this book if nothing is new? The answer is that, although the economic forces haven't changed, the understanding of how these forces will act to shape the Internet and commerce on the Internet is still quite incomplete. In the pages that follow I hope to provide some additional understanding. But not complete understanding. First, I am not in a position to know all the ways in which the Internet might impact the economy. Instead, I have focused on a few important issues with which I am familiar and have built the book around those issues.

In large part, the book applies very simple economic concepts to particular aspects of the Internet economy or, more particularly, to e-commerce, and tries to provide some insights that might prove helpful to anyone doing business, or contemplating doing business, where the Internet might play a role.

Additionally, the book tries to answer some questions that are somewhat more academic in nature, such as why things went so very wrong with the early prognostications about the Internet. This is academic not because it is necessarily studied by academics, but because in a sense it doesn't matter. The past is the past. Still, this very recent past is an episode that many of us are unlikely to see duplicated again on the same scale in our lifetimes. It is, in and of itself, an interesting story. The book doesn't focus on the history per se, but instead focuses on understanding why financial events went so awry.

Even though the Internet-stock collapse has brought forth a resurgence of Internet skepticism, a logical framework to replace the previous thinking about Internet business strategy has yet to take hold. Companies still need to determine how to incorporate the Internet into their business models. Even with so many of the first generation of Internet companies crashing and burning, and with Internet stock market valuations now so much reduced, the Internet is going to be an important tool, and business managers need to understand the economic forces at work in Internet-based markets.

Many of the prognostications about the Internet—rapidly increasing numbers of users, rapidly increasing advertising revenues, rapidly increasing sales—fertilized wildly optimistic prognostications for the performance of Internet companies as if a virtual cornucopia of wealth were going to come streaming down upon investors in those companies (and it did for those lucky enough to get in early and leave before the deluge). But even if all the prognostications of increased use and growth in revenue had been true—as some of them were—that would not have assured the rosy financial scenario that so many investors and analysts anticipated.

One of the main focuses of this book is an examination of whether the rewards to successful technology companies, including Internet companies (yes, there will be some successful Internet companies), are going to flow almost entirely to earlybirds, with laggards lucky to get the scraps, or whether this view, otherwise known as first-mover-wins, is misplaced. This material is covered at length in chapter 3, which discusses the literature on lock-in, the economic concept that is the basis for the first-mover-wins claims. And it is the claim of first-mover-wins that dominated the thinking that eventually roiled the markets and led to the closings of so many Internet start-ups.

What You Will Find in Later Chapters

There are several major themes that run throughout the book.

The Internet is likely to change many lives and provide a great deal of new wealth to society—but that doesn't necessarily lead to above-normal profits for those who invest in Internet activities, whether the investors are companies or individuals. The idea that large technological advances must be accompanied by above-normal profits for companies wise enough to invest in these markets is not a law of economics. The optimists correctly point to the large and rapidly growing demand in such markets. But one ignores the forthcoming supply at one's peril. As has always been the case, an understanding of the interaction of supply and demand is critical to truly understanding how any market, even a high-tech market, will play out. In the long run, free entry into Internet markets can be expected to keep profits down, and in the short run, profits might be below average if there is overinvestment by companies erroneously believing that any growing industry must throw off great profits.

Investors usually do not part with their money without some explanation of why they should do so.[1] Such an explanation was forthcoming from the proponents of the Internet revolution. The intellectual underpinnings of the claims that "the Internet changes everything" derive from a belief that Internet markets were first-mover-wins, a concept that is itself derived from certain fashionable academic theories known as path dependence and lock-in. Although these theories were in vogue at leading academic institutions, they were nonetheless without any real world support. Chapter 3 analyzes the claim that technology markets are first-mover-wins.

As I explain in chapter 3, the often-cited "network effects" will usually be minor for most business conducted on the Internet. Contrary to common misconceptions, network effects do not come about just because business is conducted on a network. Nor are economies of scale likely to be greatly enhanced for most e-commerce companies. Yet, without these preconditions, winner-take-all results will be no more likely for Internet incarnations of these industries than for their bricks-and-mortar counterparts. And if markets are not winner-take-all, then being first should impart no extra advantage relative to bricks-and-mortar versions of these industries.

But even when markets are winner-take-all, that doesn't translate into first-mover-wins. The idea that companies must be willing to sacrifice almost everything, including quality, so as to get to market first was constantly repeated during the Internet heyday, but incessant repetition does not make it true. Everything else being equal, being first usually does provide some advantage, whether we are talking about bricks-and-mortar companies or Internet companies. But everything else rarely *is* equal, and the advice from Internet gurus telling people to get to market first so as to lock in customers was not correct. In chapter 3 I explain why these theories were wrong.

Online retailing provides convenience and benefits to consumers—it is fast, it is easy to search and compare prices, and you can shop from your living room. But not everything can be easily sold on the Internet.

Chapter 4 delineates the conditions under which selling over the Internet makes sense; given those conditions, it is likely that only a minority of industries will find the Internet to be their primary mode of operation. The belief that practically anything—

from dog food to potatoes—could be successfully sold by virtual companies on the Internet ignored, among other things, the nature of the evolution of many industries in achieving greater efficiency in such mundane matters as distribution and logistics. It also ignored the fact that, for many—perhaps most—products, consumers will prefer bricks-and-mortar retailers with their dressing rooms, instant gratification, fast return of merchandise, and other characteristics that will never be imitated in the virtual world. One of the themes that will recur several times is that old-time competitive industries are usually very good at what they do, and starry-eyed, well-funded newcomers fresh from MBA programs are unlikely to be able to compete, either in the knowledge they bring or in overall competence. Lack of respect for established players and business methods was a major shortcoming of Internet start-ups.

Still, some products should do well being sold on the Internet and in Chapter 4 I examine which products those might be. I also examine the nature of Internet pricing and whether auction-based selling is really the form of selling that makes the most sense. There are good economic reasons that retailing has evolved the way it has, and auctions, because they are a step backward in that evolution, are not going to become the dominant form of pricing. Auctions only make sense for odd lots, surplus, one-of-a-kind items, or items for which the audience likes the thrill of the chase.

E-commerce companies do not need to expend resources on physical stores, providing them with what should be a cost advantage over their bricks-and-mortar counterparts. But this does not imply that Internet companies will be more profitable than their higher-priced bricks-and-mortar versions. Chapter 5 explores the manner in which profits are generated long-term and concludes that the future is not bright for easy profits on the Internet. Above-normal profits are normally due to a lack of competition. The Internet, with its free entry, would be expected to promote competition, which is good for consumers but bad for producers.

Given the cost structure of Internet companies, one would expect that their advantage will actually lead to lower margins, as they are normally measured, not the higher margins that were envisioned by most commentators. The problem with the high-margin claim is its implicit assertion that competition will occur chiefly between Internet companies on the one hand and bricks-and-mortar companies on the other. In reality, Internet companies will compete largely with other Internet companies, and bricks-and-mortar companies will compete largely with one another. Therefore, even if online retailers have lower costs than bricks-and-mortar retailers, it is inappropriate to conclude that online retailers will be more profitable—in fact, we would expect quite the opposite.

One of the early surprises with Internet enterprises was the choice by many Web sites to model themselves on the broadcast television industry, which is entirely advertising-based. Earlier prognostications had assumed that subscription fees would be the primary form of revenue generation. In chapter 6, I examine the choice of broadcast television as the model for Internet sites. A model that includes both advertising and subscriptions easily beats an advertising-only model and is the model most commonly used in other parts of the economy. Further, while online advertising does allow very precise targeting of advertisements and immediate feedback on the impacts of the advertising, thus enhancing the ability of Internet sites to raise revenues, there doesn't seem to be much room for Internet advertising to grow since the current advertising revenues appear to be higher than can be justified when compared to other media. Therefore, Internet advertising will not generate sufficient dollars to support the many Web sites that were hoping to pay for content with it.

Chapter 7 contains a lengthy discussion of the sale of music and other copyrighted material on the Internet. This is an issue that has been much in the news, and the sale of music and other digital products promises to be one of the largest and most successful venues for Internet sales. I take the reader on an extended review of the impacts of copying, including a history of previous instances when the owners of copyright have cried wolf about their demise, only to be proved wrong by experience. I move on to the current arguments about the impacts of the Internet and the evidence surrounding the Napster case. I also explain how record companies might have made an important tactical mistake in shutting down Napster since new technologies based on protocols such as Gnutella are likely to be a more fearsome threat to copyright owners.

Chapter 7 also discusses new technologies known as digital rights management. These technologies are viewed with great suspicion by many analysts who view them as providing far too much power to the sellers and possibly engendering a diminution of free speech. My analysis, however, suggests that these fears are unwarranted.

Finally, the overriding myth of the Internet frenzy was that the laws of supply and demand did not apply to the Internet. My goal, when the reader has finished the book, is to have illustrated that economic laws transcend changes in technology. I would go so far as to say that they will apply to all markets at all times, since I am confident I will not be proven wrong in my lifetime. Nevertheless, care needs to be taken in using economic concepts. Even economists can get carried away with trendy ideas and forget to use scientific methods in judging theories. There is an important lesson here because the abandonment of sound economic principles in favor of faddish impulses has the potential to cause great damage to the economy.

Notes

1. Economists argue about whether certain events, such as tulipmania in Holland, a famous seventeenth-century instance of skyrocketing tulip prices that on the surface appeared to bear little semblance to sanity, were actually instances of financial "bubbles." Economic models generally claim that bubbles exist when investors acknowledge no fundamental reason for high prices but invest anyway in the expectation that prices will rise. In other words, these models put

forward a form of the "greater fool" family of theories that has investors operating on the assumption that others (the greater fools although not necessarily motley ones) will be left holding the bag. The definition of a bubble in this literature is that prices are high only because prices are expected to be high, not because there is an inherently "foolish" reason put forward that nonetheless seduces some investors. The fact that investments may appear foolish—to almost all in hindsight and to many during the event—is not evidence of a bubble, at least not in the economics literature. Thus there is likely to be a disconnect between economists and noneconomists, the latter being most likely to consider a bubble to exist whenever large numbers of investors bet incorrectly and in a very big way on unproven theories. See the symposium on bubbles in the *Journal of Economic Perspectives*, 4, no. 2 (Spring 1990): 13–102.

Chapter 2

Basic Economics of the Internet

This chapter introduces the reader to some basic economic concepts. First, the manner in which the Internet creates value is explored. Then several concepts often related to the Internet are examined. These are the concepts of winner-take-all, first-mover-wins, network effects, and instant scalability.

How the Internet Creates Value

The Internet creates value by reducing the costs of transmitting information. That, in a nutshell, is all the Internet does. I put it this way not to belittle what the Internet accomplishes. After all, automobiles and airplanes merely lowered the costs of transportation, and language merely lowers the cost of communication, though all are monumental achievements. But it is important to strip myth away from reality. Information transmission is very important. The Internet is a terrific advance in lowering the cost of information. But—and this is most important—information transmission does not change the laws of economics.

Transmitting information is one of the most valuable functions in an economy. But it is useful to contrast the Internet with other technologies that have reduced the cost of transmitting information, namely telephones and television.

Telephones allowed instantaneous voice communication, whereas the technologies prior to the telephone allowed very slow written communications via mail or faster, but limited, communication via the telegraph and Morse code. The telegraph never made it into private homes, so communication using telegraphs required delivery of telegrams. Thus, while it virtually eliminated the time to move the message from one city to another, it still required a costly and time-consuming local delivery.

The telephone, therefore, was a tremendous improvement, in large part because it was intended to be used in homes and businesses, eliminating any delivery costs whatsoever. It required the building of a new and very costly infrastructure—the ubiquitous telephone lines that cover the landscape and the wires leading into and through homes. This tremendous investment retarded its diffusion, but the value was so great that the diffusion became virtually complete, and telephony completely transformed communication as it was then known.

Television, and radio before it, had a somewhat different impact. Television offers one-way communication. Information, along with entertainment, is transmitted from broadcasting studios to consumers who possess television or radio receivers.

What were the precursors to radio and television? Live entertainment, theatrical releases of movies, and, in the home, a fledgling phonograph industry. Television and radio greatly enhanced the choices available to consumers. These technologies brought entertainment into the home and the automobile. They greatly magnified the size of the audience that could enjoy any given performance, whether by a singer, a comedian, or an actor. They allowed the virtually instantaneous transmission of news and information.

How does the Internet compare? It is based largely on the same transmission mechanism as cable television and telephones, two prior technologies capable of going into people's homes and offices. The reception is largely confined to computers, which needed only minor modifications to provide Internet access. Although broadband required serious new investment in infrastructure, much of the infrastructure was already in place, and much of the new infrastructure can be thought of as more of an upgrade than a brand new investment. So the Internet is more evolutionary, in terms of infrastructure, than were radio and television, which required new transmitters, cameras, and receiving equipment.

As far as content is concerned, the Internet is also less revolutionary. It allows for two-way communication, entertainment, and information. So far, it doesn't sound like much of an advance since televisions, radios, and telephones, taken together, did the same things. What distinguishes the Internet from the prior technologies, however, is its ability to quickly retrieve information stored on computers, something that telephones and television can't do. Television can't because it is a one-way medium. Telephones can't because they are analog devices intended to have sound come out the speaker of the receiving end, and users are not computers that can "remember" information and manipulate it as it comes across the line.[1]

By combining the two-way transmission mechanism of the telephone with the informational display of the television and the database capability of computers, the Internet does provide a new experience. The crude intelligence of computers, which will only improve over time, can be used to tailor information to specific users or needs. Users can quickly find information and retrieve it for instantaneous or later use. Some of the uses are extraordinary while others are quite mundane.

In the extraordinary category is the ability to participate in virtual worlds with other individuals who lose their true identities and can take on the identities they wish. Or the ability to search for any of hundreds of thousands of used items for sale on eBay. Information is available in unprecedented simplicity, unprecedented quantity, and unprecedented variety.

On a more mundane level, the Internet can be used to help organize our Saturday nights. If I want to listen to music, I can catch an Internet broadcast instead of an over-the-air broadcast. The same will eventually be true for video. If I wish, I can find someone to date, with a set of characteristics that I specify, and also look at her pictures and read her biography. Nothing that wasn't available before the Internet, but before the Internet it required a far greater expenditure of money and time. If I want to know what movies are playing nearby, as well as starting times and reviews, I can go online. Newspapers provide some of the same services, but you are limited there to but a single review, or perhaps to a summary of reviews, since space limitations restrict the ability of the newspaper to provide the full set of previous reviews. The telephone can be used to find out what is playing, to find out if the movie is sold out, and get the starting times and prices, but reviews are not available. Is this combination of newspaper and telephone that the Internet provides revolutionary or evolutionary?

These improvements certainly aren't earthshaking, but if you multiply these values by the thousand little ways that the Internet can provide more information faster, you have a considerable improvement in people's lives.

In a similar vein, companies can keep track of customers' orders, their consumption habits, credit history, and so forth in a seamless and cohesive fashion. Marketers can have a field day. Paranoids can have more sleepless nights over the misuse of information. Politicians have new topics on which to hold hearings.

But all is not necessarily good for those companies attempting to do business using the Internet. The reduction in transmission costs, while creating value, should reduce the ability of companies participating on the Internet to take advantage of what we would otherwise call "locational" monopolies, the monopoly resulting from being physically close to the customers. Less clear is the impact on brand-name loyalty. The Web makes it very easy to explore new locations and to get feedback on those Web locations. This should ease entry since incumbents would be thought harder pressed to take advantage of consumer ignorance and inertia than they might in the bricks-and-mortar world. One might also think that it will be more difficult for price spreads to exist, and for companies to engage in differential pricing since consumers should be able to do price comparisons at lower costs. Ratings on the reliability of retailers can be determined with the click of a mouse.

If, on the one hand, these improvements in retrieving information come to pass, we can expect profitability of Internet companies to be affected—negatively. Companies that are outstanding, however, should rise to prominence more rapidly. On the other hand, many consumers tire of providing their credit card information over and over again and tend to stay with one or two sites instead of continuously trying new ones. If this behavior is similar enough to what one finds in the bricks-and-mortar world, then the performance of Internet companies may not be all that different from their bricks-and-mortar counterparts.

Special Economics of the Internet—
or Maybe Not So Special

Network Effects

Many products and companies associated with the Internet are thought to have an economic property known as network effects.[2] As we will see, some products actually do have these effects, but many products that were involved in some way with e-commerce do not have even the slightest trace of network effects. Nevertheless, many business models applied to e-commerce were often based on unsupported and ultimately incorrect assumptions that ALL of e-commerce was subject to powerful network effects. How much of the recent Internet meltdown can be laid at the doorstep of these mistaken business strategies cannot be ascertained with any precision, but a substantial portion of the damage can certainly be attributed to them.

The technical definition of network effects is fairly straightforward. Network effects are present when a product becomes more useful to consumers in proportion to the number of other people using it.[3] For example, the owner of a fax machine benefits from the fact that there are lots of other people with fax machines. If there were no other users of fax machines, you couldn't send a fax to anyone, and it would best be used as a doorstop. Obviously, telephone and other literal networks where users are physically linked to one another exhibit network effects. Less obvious are what have been called virtual networks, such as the network of WordPerfect users.[4] It might be that some, or even most, of the users of WordPerfect care about the number of other users. If WordPerfect users paid more for their copy of WordPerfect as the number of other WordPerfect users increased, then WordPerfect would be said to embody network effects.

Note that there need not be anything particularly high-tech about network effects. Automobile owners benefit from having a ready supply of parts and mechanics that makes it easier to have their cars repaired should they break down. The more units there are of a particular automobile model, the more likely it is that any single owner can find such repair facilities. Therefore, to the extent that consumers value the ease of repair, automobiles should have network effects. The same would be true for almost any product that might break.

Network effects clearly exist, but their strength is often overestimated. Why is an overestimation of network effects so dangerous to the thinking of business managers? The answer has to do with business strategies that have been propounded based on network effects. These are theories that exhort companies to take advantage of network effects to lock in winning positions. These are theories that suggest that getting to market first and generating a large market share and installed base is of the utmost importance. These are theories that imply that losing money to gain sales and share is a worthwhile investment because companies that succeed in generating large sales will have easy sailing in the future with their customers locked into their products. These are theories that make claims that are inconsistent with the way markets have actually worked.

Before examining how those theories have been translated into business strategies, which forms the basis of chapter 3, we need to examine several other economic concepts that are closely related and that are, in many cases, more important than network effects.

Economies of Scale

Economies of scale, a concept that has been taught in microeconomics classes for many generations, implies that average costs decrease as the company sells more and gets larger. Note that we are talking about average costs. Average costs are simply total costs divided by the number of units sold. Automobile companies experience significant economies of scale, which is one reason that a Rolls-Royce costs more to make than a Cadillac. There are large start-up costs, more formally known as fixed costs, in designing a new automobile and in creating all the dies and assembly facilities to produce a particular model of a car. Almost all manufacturing exhibits some economies of scale. But usually, at some point, these economies tend to run out and are superseded by other components of production costs that raise the average cost of production as output increases.

Many new high-tech products are thought to have very significant economies of scale because they have very large start-up costs. When a software product is developed, for example, the total cost of development is a fixed cost that does not depend on whether ten or ten million units are actually sold. The costs of duplicating, shipping, and servicing units that eventually land in the hands of consumers are often considered to be close to zero, a convenient, though not necessarily accurate, assumption.[5]

Still, it seems likely that software, microprocessors, and many other high-tech products do have substantial economies of scale. Although this concept has been given a role in business strategies that is far inferior to that of network effects, economies of scale are likely to have very similar impacts to network effects, and are frequently going to be more significant than network effects. Their somewhat neglected role in recent economic literature is probably due to the fact that the concept of economies to scale is not new and doesn't seem as sexy to academics who usually are looking for something new, even if it is just a new label on an old concept.[6]

Winner-Take-All

Network effects and economies of scale have almost identical impacts. Each works to the advantage of large companies over small ones. Large networks, by definition, have stronger network effects than do small networks, meaning that, everything else being equal, consumers should be willing to pay more to join a large network. This should enhance the profitability of the large network relative to the small network. Similarly, economies of scale imply that large companies have lower costs than do small companies, thus providing them with larger profits. In terms of outcomes, these two economic forces are virtually indistinguishable from one another since each provides an advantage to large companies and networks relative to their smaller rivals.

This advantage of large over small is sometimes referred to as increasing returns (to scale). Increasing returns was normally thought to lead to winner-take-all results, particularly when products from different vendors were considered to be identical, as economic theories often model them to be. Some modern versions of this story, nodding to the reality that market shares are almost never 100 percent, prefer the term "winner-take-most." I see no need to mince words and will use the more exciting if less accurate terminology.

Increasing returns, therefore, was inconsistent with the ideal of having many competitors in the market, one of the fundamental assumptions in economists' basic model of competition. It was also inconsistent with the observation that many industries had far more than a single dominant company. For these and other reasons, the concept of increasing returns was historically relegated to a relatively obscure position in economic analysis.[7]

Whenever large companies enjoy cost advantages that smaller

companies do not, a winner-take-all outcome can result. But it need not, particularly if products are different from one another and appeal to different types of consumers. That is why the video format for camcorders (hi-8, before the advent of digital video camcorders) has mainly been different from the VHS format for VCRs. VHS was successful against Beta in large part due to the longer playing time afforded by its larger cassette. The large cassette proved to be a disadvantage in the camcorder market where portability was very important.[8]

Of course, many companies with large market shares, such as Packard-Bell in computers or General Motors in automobile manufacturing, did not have the cost advantages over their rivals that was expected of large companies. But, for some reason, this possibility was thought not to apply to Internet companies. Morgan Stanley opined in a 1999 report:

> Owing in part to economics of increasing returns, the revenue/profit streams that accrue, in time, to the Internet leaders (defined as companies with the most/stickiest customers) should be broad-based and recurring and the user reach supported by the leaders may be impressive (of Microsoft-ian and ATT-ian proportions, or higher).[9]

This type of thinking led to Waterloo-ian results, but I will return to that later.

Nonetheless, there is yet one more factor that can also lead to winner-take-all results—instant scalability. Instant scalability is the ability of a company to meet market demand in almost no time, tending to cause any favored product to get the lion's share of the market. Instant scalability arises when the production process requires non-specific inputs. For example, the production of copies of a piece of software such a Quicken or Word requires disk duplication machinery (or Web servers for software downloads). The machines that make copies of CDs are the same no matter what is on the CD being copied. Thus a machine making copies of

Word could almost instantaneously be converted to start making copies of Quicken. Therefore, if demand shifts to favor one product over another, the facilities exist to very quickly start making copies of the now popular product. Note that this is not the same as saying that the cost of duplication is near zero. It could cost a million dollars for each CD (e.g., if the materials in a CD were very expensive), but the concept would still be the same, and instant scalability would still exist in the industry.

Unlike economies of scale and network effects, instant scalability does not necessarily lead to winner-take-all results. If consumers do not uniformly agree that one product in the market is superior to the others (in terms of bang for the buck), instant scalability will not lead to dominant market shares. For many information-based products, however, there will be fairly general agreement among consumers about product quality, and large market shares will prevail. A common example of long standing can be found in the movie industry where in any given week one or two movies tend to take in a majority of box-office receipts. Theaters, projectors, and movie duplication equipment are non-specialized, which has allowed these high shares to exist even though they tend to be very short-lived.

Whether a company's production has the characteristics of economies of scale, network effects, or instant scalability depends on the specifics of its products and the manner in which it conducts business. The exact manner in which it uses or does not use the Internet can also determine the existence or nonexistence of these economic characteristics. One has to examine each industry on a case-by-case basis to determine whether winner-take-all is a likely result. For our purposes here, however, the question is more specifically how using the Internet might alter these characteristics for businesses. I turn to that now.

How the Internet Alters the Likelihood of Winner-Take-All

Many computer products, such as software and central processing chips, seem to have winner-take-all characteristics. For instance, we find ourselves with one dominant operating system (Windows), one dominant spreadsheet (Excel), one dominant financial package (Quicken), one dominant chip maker (Intel), and so on.

It is sometimes thought that all technology companies, usually defined to include Internet-based companies, have this characteristic. A typical view is the following:

> Because technology is such a dynamic area, tech companies' fortunes—and the market's assessments of those fortunes—change rapidly, and none faster than in the Internet area. "Most of these are winner-take-most or winner-take-all markets," says Michael Mauboussin, chief investment strategist at Credit Suisse First Boston.[10]

Other industries seem somewhat less prone to winner-take-all. The leading brand of television, computer, hotdog, or grocery store usually has a market share of less than 50 percent, even though that share may be quite large. Companies in these latter industries are usually thought to exhibit decreasing returns, meaning that at some point getting larger starts disadvantaging the company relative to its competitors. Although the leading companies in these industries may have quite large market shares, they are not thought to exhibit economies of scale or network effects.

. Could use of the Internet, or the transformation of a business model from bricks-and-mortar to Internet-based, turn an industry that was previously not winner-take-all into one that is? This is really the central question in trying to understand how the embrace of the Internet will alter results in industries not previously thought to have increasing returns. What might be the expected impact of converting a bricks-and-mortar company into one that uses the Internet to do business?

The creation of the Web site is a fixed cost, so this component of cost might produce an economy of scale effect. But if the cost of Web-site creation is small relative to other costs such as warehousing, shipping, production, sales, customer relations, and so forth, then the fixed cost of Web-site creation is unlikely to result in much of a scale economy and thus unlikely to result in winner-take-all.

It is commonly thought that most companies operating on the Internet are subject to network effects, presumably because the Internet itself is a network.[11] This would seem naturally to lead to the conclusion that most e-commerce will be winner-takes-all.

This view is mistaken for a great number of companies classified as Internet companies, perhaps even a majority. The source of this error is due to a misunderstanding of network effects. Many Internet companies, when properly analyzed, are seen to have few if any network effects—Amazon, Etoys, PeaPod, Priceline, and most other Internet retailers have (or had, since these companies are disappearing like flies) no new network effects not found in bricks-and-mortar counterparts. Others companies, such as eBay with its online auctions of used products, and the various Internet Messaging services by the likes of AOL, Yahoo, and Microsoft, do have strong network effects, but they seem to be more the exception than the rule for Internet companies.

Buyers will tend to flock to auction markets, such as eBay, which have the largest number of items for sale since a consumer is more likely to find what he is looking for, especially used and obscure items, if many items are being sold. Similarly, sellers will prefer to have the broadest possible exposure to buyers. Since information is the key to these markets, there is every reason to believe that Internet sellers of used items will come to dominate the market, besting the classifieds found in most newspapers.

Of course, the auction component is largely irrelevant to this network effect. The auction offers an aura of excitement and automates what is often an unpleasant bargaining experience, but if all the sellers on eBay were to have just offered their products for sale at fixed prices, eBay would likely still have done very well. We will return to the role of auctions in the section "What About Auctions?" in chapter 4.

Markets where interaction among consumers is important are also likely candidates for strong network effects. One example of this is a site such as GeoCities with its virtual communities. In these cases, users of the services want to have a variety of topics and of people to talk with; their valuation therefore depends on the number of other users. These are circumstances where strong network effects might in turn lend themselves to winner-take-all outcomes. Instant messaging, such as AOL Instant Messaging, or Microsoft or Yahoo Messaging, has strong literal network effects and without interoperability will likely evolve into a winner-take-all result. Of course, consumers will prefer interoperability, and it is likely that AOL, which has been trying to prevent this, will have to cave in to the will of its consumers if its rivals can establish a large enough beachhead to cause AOL's customers to seriously object to their reduced ability to communicate with non-AOL users.[12]

But the majority of Internet companies do not have strong network effects. Certainly this is true for almost all online retailing. Whether we are talking about selling sirloin steaks, Furbys, or Elvis recordings, the value of the retailing services to individual consumers bears no relationship to the number of consumers serviced by the online sellers.

What is noteworthy in all this is that there are important branches of e-commerce, perhaps the majority of e-commerce activities, that do not exhibit much in the way of network effects. Take the case of someone shopping for toys on the Internet. That consumer is likely to have very little interest in the number of other toy shoppers that will patronize a particular Web e-tailer. Why should they? They want to buy the most appropriate products at the best price. Very little of that decision will depend on the number of other consumers patronizing a particular retailer. One exception to this, but one that I believe is a minor exception, is product reviews listed on the Web site. One of the clever features of Amazon is its listing of product reviews that are conveniently accessible to users contemplating the purchase of a product. Compare the number of reviews on Amazon to that on Barnes and Noble's Web site. Amazon seems to understand better that reviews are one of the few network features it can provide its customers.

But even this is a weak network effect since consumers can go to Amazon to get the product reviews and then go to another site that might have lower prices to make the actual purchase. In other words, other Web sites can "free-ride" on Amazon's product reviews, limiting the value of the reviews as network effects. Consumers cannot free-ride on real network effects such as AOL's Instant Messenger. If you want to have access to the many individuals who use the AOL product, you can only do so using the AOL product. AOL has fought hard to limit interoperability that would allow users of other instant messaging programs access to the large AOL Messaging subscriber base in order to keep the network effects for itself.[13, 14]

Customers of most Internet retailers will be interested in the same general factors that they care about in the bricks-and-mortar universe—price, return policy, whether the item is in stock, the company's reputation for reliability, and so forth. The fact that business is taking place on the Internet does not introduce winner-take-all characteristics into these markets. There is no reason to think that the biggest toy e-tailer would have a more significant advantage over other Internet toy stores than large bricks-and-mortar toy stores have over their smaller competitors. Of course, if the bricks-and-mortar world is winner-take-all, we might expect the Internet version of this industry to be the same.

Notes

1. Of course, telephones can be hooked up to modems, but this is essentially a close cousin of the Internet, if not exactly the Internet itself.

2. See Michael L. Katz and Carl Shapiro, "Network Externalities, Competition, and Compatibility," *American Economic Review*, 75:3 (June

1985): 424–440 and Stan Liebowitz and Stephen E. Margolis, "Network Effects and Externalities," entry in *The New Palgrave's Dictionary of Economics and the Law*, vol. 2 (New York: Macmillan, 1998), pp. 671–675.

3. Actually, network effects can be either positive or negative, meaning that the value consumers receive goes up or down as the number of other users changes. As more telephone users clog the lines, the network effects become negative. As the term has been used in the literature, however, network effects are almost invariably positive.

4. This terminology is based on Liebowitz and Margolis, "Network Effects" entry in the *Handbook of Telecommunications Economics*, M. Cave, S. Majumdar, and I. Vogelsang (eds.), Elsevier, 2002.

5. The assumption is pedagogically convenient if one wishes to illustrate the workings of average costs and economies of scale. It is theoretically convenient if one wishes to characterize the software industry as a natural monopoly without going to the trouble of examining the actual costs of support, shipping, and duplicating.

6. Of course, even network effects are not terribly new. A reader of current economic literature might be forgiven for thinking that the concept of network effects emerged de novo in the mid-1980s with the paper by Katz and Shapiro. In fact, these concepts had been around since at least the 1950s in a then influential paper by Harvey Leibenstein, "Bandwagon, Snob, and Veblen Effects in the Theory of Consumer's Demand," *Quarterly Journal of Economics* 64 (1950): 183–207.

7. This concept has recently enjoyed a surge in popularity in several fields of economics. Our interest is in the usage found in the fields of industrial organization and economic history, where Brian Arthur and Paul David have played important roles. See Paul Krugman's writings in *Slate*, discussed in footnote 11 in chapter 3, for more details.

8. See the discussion in the section of chapter 3 entitled "What Does the Real World Tell Us About Strong Lock-In?"

9. Page 3 of slide show *The Internet Company Handbook*, June 1999, Morgan Stanley Dean Witter. It can be found here: *http://www. morganstanley.com/techresearch/netcomhdbook/ih6.pdf*

10. Greg Ip and E. S. Browning, "Nasdaq Swings Are Unprecedented but Consumers Are Not Spooked," *Wall Street Journal* (online edition), April 14, 2000.

11. See the reference in chapter 8 to the article by Thomas Petzinger, which nicely illustrates this point.

12. Of course, if users are willing to put up with multiple programs on their computers, which might not be all that much of an inconvenience, these various messaging services can easily coexist.

13. Reshma Kapadia, "AOL-Lotus deal doesn't satisfy rivals: Critics say tests do little to move toward IM interoperatibility." By Reuters, New York, Aug. 15.

14. Although these services are currently free, the competitors believe that these services will somehow provide sufficient profits to warrant their current investment.

Chapter 3

Racing to Be First
Faddish and Foolish

Pundits and professors told Internet entrepreneurs to race to get a large presence in Internet space. This might have been good advice if these markets had first-mover-wins characteristics. Forgoing short-term profits for short-term market share increases would make sense if these market shares were later converted into long-term profit gains. Most Internet markets, however, did not have first-mover-wins characteristics. Why did so many believe that technology industries had the characteristics of first-mover-wins? This chapter reveals the faulty analysis underlying these beliefs.

> *The ideas of economists and political philosophers, both when they are right and when they are wrong, are more powerful than is commonly understood. Indeed the world is ruled by little else. Practical men, who believe themselves to be quite exempt from any intellectual influence, are usually the slaves of some defunct economist.*
>
> John Maynard Keynes

It is often asserted that being first is of paramount importance in the Internet age, far more important than it is for bricks-and-mortar industries. For example, Mary Meeker, the famous, or now infamous, Morgan Stanley stock-market analyst closely associated with the Nasdaq and Internet stock run-ups, said in a 1997 report:

> Our Internet team thinks first-mover advantage for Web retailers may be important. The retail group, by contrast, doesn't think being first matters much, since barriers to entry will likely remain low on the Web.[1]

What caused the Internet group to believe that first-mover-wins was an apt description of Internet retailing? What led the Internet group astray? Stock-market analysts usually do not create their own theories—they lack the training to do so. Instead, as Keynes wrote, they usually take ideas, right or wrong, from some academic thinker, as indicated in the following January 1998 quotation from a stock market analyst (my italics):

> The notion of "first-mover advantage" is gaining currency quickly and, in turn, influencing companies' chances for success. . . . The idea of first-mover advantage seems to have become fashionable only recently. In a Dow Jones database search, the term appears 156 times in publications since the beginning of 1998, but only 28 times in the six years from 1988 through 1993. Much of its usage, before the rise of the Internet, *was in overseas business publications and academic journals.*[2]

The idea of first-mover-wins fits in neatly with a strain of economic thought that arose in the late 1980s and was nurtured, incubated, and proselytized to business audiences by academics with theories that may soon be, but are not yet, defunct. That is the subject of the next few sections.

From Winner-Take-All to First-Mover-Wins

If the market is going to become dominated by a small number of companies, perhaps as few as one, how does a company get to be that top dog? The typical answer has been: "Get established first. At any cost."

This idea that being first is essential is a truly pernicious bit of faux wisdom; it has helped companies throw themselves madly off a cliff like lemmings, thinking they were bound for glory. I do not wish to split hairs over the first-mover versus, say, a second-mover a week later, for that is a distinction without a difference.[3] It is really the idea that early movers have a large lead over later movers that deserves a good part of the blame for appearing to give credence to these misguided business plans of the e-commerce companies.

Finding examples of this view is easy. In a typical story of the time, a company founder and chief technology officer is quoted in the *Wall Street Journal* stating "Our biggest competitor is time—being the first to market with this product."[4]

The generality of this claim is nicely illustrated in a column in eCompany (each of the companies mentioned in the quote soon went belly-up):

> "We have the first-mover advantage," Women.com CEO Marleen McDaniel told CNBC in June 1999. "They have the first-mover advantage," a Zona Research analyst told a reporter, explaining why eToys's stock was a steal. "Eve. com is an outstanding e-commerce opportunity with a first-mover advantage," Idealab founder Bill Gross bragged in a press release. As Draper Fisher Jurvetson partner Tim Draper told *USA Today* in October 1999, the first-mover is "usually the (company) that's going to win it."[5]

Or this from *Information Rules*, in many respects one of the more reasonable books of advice for the information economy:

> First-mover advantages can be powerful and long-lasting in lock-in markets, especially those in information indus-

tries where scale economies are substantial. If you can establish an installed base before the competition arrives on the scene, you may make it difficult for later entrants to achieve the scale economies necessary to compete.[6]

Of course, as proper academics, Professors Shapiro and Varian, the authors of *Information Rules,* are somewhat circumspect about overstating the advantages of being first. They do not say that being first *does* ensure an advantage, only that it *might.* Still, for a business audience that finds sufficiently deep meaning in books such as *Who Moved My Cheese?* to keep it on top of the bestseller list for years, these nuances are likely to be unnoticed. Furthermore, in the "Lessons" section of their chapter 6, which is where many busy readers are likely to gain their insights, we find the less circumspect sentences: "Be prepared to invest to build an installed base through promotions and by offering up-front discounts. You can't succeed in competitive lock-in markets without making these investments." Perhaps an overzealous editor put "can't" where "might not" had originally been so as to put a little more punch in the statement, but to a typical business reader, it would certainly appear that one needs to lose money initially in order to gain the ever-so-important market share.

More exuberant still is Kevin Kelly in his book *New Rules for a New Economy.* Not only should you discount your product to get market share, Kelly tells businesspeople, but you need to actually give it away. He has ten cutely named "rules" (chapters) in his book, the fourth of which is "Follow the Free." Here is a sampling:

> As crackpot as it sounds, in the distant future nearly everything we make will (at least for a short while) be given away free—refrigerators, skis, laser projectors, clothes, you name it.[7]

> Talk of generosity, of information that wants to be free, and of virtual communities is often dismissed by businesspeople as youthful new age idealism. It may be

idealistic but it is also the only sane way to launch a commercial economy in the emerging space.[8]

At least Kelly understood that giving nearly everything away sounded like a crackpot idea. The problem was that he didn't seem to understand that what he was putting forward didn't just *sound* like a crackpot idea but actually *was* a crackpot idea. That is not to deny that giving a product away may sometimes make sense. Free samples have been around forever. But the talk of information wanting to be free is nonsense. And the idea that refrigerators, laser projectors, and clothing will be given away, as if the network effects could possibly be large enough to warrant giving away these products, indicates a serious misunderstanding of the importance of network effects (even if chips were sewn in every pocket). Kelly's advice is grossly overstated at best and has since been proven wrong when the result is to produce astronomical losses on the balance sheet with no chance of making enough profit down the road to provide a normal return.

Last, but not least, we have Professor Brian Arthur, the pied piper of lock-in. Arthur has received near-universal adoration from the media for his articulation of lock-in and his claims of having reinvented increasing returns (concepts I will discuss in the next section).[9] Arthur tells business strategists in a 1998 *Harvard Business Review* article (see note 18): "Two maxims are widely accepted in knowledge-based markets: it pays to hit the market first, and it pays to have superb technology." Yet that same year he discarded even the importance of having good technology in an interview with Booze-Allen & Hamilton:

If you are in a technically based industry, then it's not sufficient to think in terms of lowering your cost, improving your quality, keeping products moving out the door. That's the traditional challenge for what I call the bulk manufacturing economy. But in high tech, that's no longer sufficient. If these markets are unstable, they can lock in to something and become dominated.

In that case, business strategy has to go far beyond the usual adages about costs down, quality up, core competency. High tech adds a new layer of complication. You have to allow that you are playing games where the winner can walk off with a great deal of the market and the losers are left with practically nothing, even if their products are technically brilliant, and the cost is right. So basically the strategies are very much the strategies you would apply in presidential primaries. You want to build up market share, you want to build up user base. If you do, you can lock in that market.[10]

So there you have it. Technical brilliance, low prices, and high quality are insufficiently important to lead to success. So much for the world beating a path to your door because you have built a better mousetrap. What could Emerson possibly have to tell us in our modern times? Instead, the winner might have mundane products, so-so quality, and high prices. But this second-rate company wins because it got to the starting line first and locked in its customers, at least as Arthur tells it.

Arthur has not been shy about claiming that traditional economic concepts were not relevant to high-technology markets.[11] Other economists, however, were less willing to throw out the old, even as they brought in the new.[12]

Where are the intellectual underpinnings for this notion of the benefits of early entry? The answer has to do with the concept of lock-in, a relatively new concept in economists' thinking. It certainly played an important role in the thinking of academics such as Arthur and Shapiro and Varian. Technology writers, such as Kevin Kelly, then ran (or perhaps flew) with these ideas.

The Concept of Lock-In

In winner-take-all markets, it is possible that there will be swift leadership changes whenever a better challenger enters the market. Lock-in, however, suggests otherwise. The winner not only takes all, he keeps taking it, even in the face of a better rival. In this view of markets, if the initial entrant gets the largest market share, lock-in will then work to keep the company's customers immobile and the company entrenched in the leading position.[13]

In the telling of the lock-in story, network effects play the key role. Network effects lead to winner-take-all, and once the winner is established, network effects keep competitors at bay. Just why this would be so has to do with a particular type of coordination problem described in the section "Strong Lock-In" below. Although the literature focuses on network effects, economies of scale could have been used instead since economies of scale also imply a winner-take-all result.[14]

Compatibility is crucially related to lock-in concepts. Whenever consumers attempt to determine which brand or type of product to buy, they must (consciously or not) go through several internal calculations. Typically, they will compare the prices and qualities of the products. They need to determine the costs of learning how to use a new product. And in network markets they also have to take account of the strength or size of the competing networks in order to gauge the size of the network effects that will be associated with the competing products. For example, in the early 1980s, a consumer determining whether to buy a VHS or Beta VCR normally considered the prospective size of the two networks.

It is this need to gauge what others are doing that leads to the theoretical possibility that consumers can, in principle, get locked into a product and be seemingly unable to switch to something better. How that might work in theory is the subject of numerous economics papers. How it worked in the real world is the subject of a far smaller and, as we shall see, notably faulty literature.

Lock-in costs can themselves be classified into two different types. First, there are the costs involved with just changing to another brand or version of a product, such as relearning old habits, becoming familiar with the new product, and also possibly being able to use the new product with old work products, such as using a new word processor to read your old documents. These are the costs of being compatible with one's self.

Second, there are costs involved in possibly losing compatibility with others. This might be exemplified by someone wishing to switch from VHS to Beta and finding a dearth of prerecorded Beta movies available at the video store, or someone switching to Lotus WordPro and finding they have trouble exchanging documents with their colleagues who use Microsoft Word.

These two different factors, being compatible with one's self and being compatible with others, play an important role in understanding how lock-in works. And these two factors are essential in delineating the crucial distinction between *weak* and *strong* forms of lock-in. The strong form of lock-in supports the concept of first-mover-wins. The weak form does not.

I must warn you that this distinction is not one that is normally made in the literature. Instead, all forms of lock-in are lumped together. Yet it is only the strong form of lock-in that leads to potential coordination problems and only the strong form of lock-in that would lead to first-mover-wins. It is a failing of this literature that it hasn't distinguished between these two types of lock-in.

It is possible to imagine a situation where a newcomer company produces a better product than an incumbent. A better product is defined as a product that a consumer would choose if he were starting from scratch and if there were no concern about compatibility, either with himself or with others. Whether that product can break into the market depends largely on the type of lock-in involved, as I now illustrate.

Strong Lock-In

A *strong* form of lock-in exists when this better product is not adopted even though the superiority of the product can overcome any self-compatibility issues for consumers. In such a case, the switch would occur if consumers didn't care about compatibility with others. Network effects, if they exist in a market, bring compatibility with other consumers to the fore and therefore the issue of whether superior products can overcome the lead of inferior incumbents has been closely associated with network effects.

Note that if the benefits of the new technology were not capable of overcoming learning costs and/or inability to use old work product, then it would be inefficient for the new technology to replace the old. These costs of learning to use new products are real costs.

Most important, if strong lock-in exists, it might be wise for sellers to try to get a large market share even if the costs of doing so are very high. That is because challengers, even those with superior products, may not be able to overcome the lead of the early birds. This is the basis for the belief in first-mover-wins.

Potential incompatibility with other users can prevent a superior challenger from vanquishing an incumbent, at least in principle. With this strong form of lock-in, even though all consumers would like to switch if enough other users would also switch, a coordination failure among users prevents consumers from actually switching. In other words, we would all like to switch, say, from VHS to Beta. Beta, let's pretend, is universally acknowledged to be better than VHS. Because each individual consumer fears that others will not switch and that, as a result, most prerecorded movies will not be available on Beta, all consumers stick with VHS. This is a case where we would all be better off making the change, but we do not make the change because we cannot coordinate our independent actions.

That is the strong-form lock-in story, and it has beguiled many an economist, particularly since at first there appeared to be some evidence to support it. It is not just a story of incompatibility with others, however. At its core, this strong-lock-in story contains an assumption that each user believes that others will continue to use the inferior product even though everyone knows that the challenger product is superior.[15]

At the time the challenger enters the market, the two types of compatibility would appear to completely favor the incumbent. Compatibility with one's old behavior imposes costs on a switch. And the incumbent, by definition, has a larger market share. However, when consumers go through a calculation about the value of switching, it would be rational for them to try to project what the future will look like. Otherwise, the first automobiles would never have been sold since there were no gas stations, and the first fax machines wouldn't have been sold since there were no faxes to receive and no one to send faxes to. It is the *expectation* of the size of the networks that actually matters. If consumers believe the challenger will do well in the market, then the market shares at the time of purchase need not be particularly relevant.

So, in fact, the importance of compatibility with others does not necessarily favor the incumbent. Challengers who are able to demonstrate the superiority of their product and gain momentum in the eyes of consumers may very well prevail, as would be required if the market were working efficiently. Therefore, it is uncertain, in theory, whether strong forms of lock-in are likely to occur.

Real-world examples of strong lock-in have been put forward, such as the typewriter keyboard or videocassette recorder format, but as I discuss below, these examples have been shown to be flat-out wrong.

It might appear that winner-take-all brought about entirely by economies of scale might also be capable of strong-form lock-in of an incumbent. After all, a new challenger, even with a better product, will have serious cost disadvantages relative to the much larger incumbent. However, the challenger has a straightforward task: investing sufficient resources to achieve a large enough scale in *new sales* so as to reach a low cost that will allow him to eventually prevail. The task facing a company trying to overcome network effects appears less simple because it requires overcoming the impacts of the *existing stock* of previous sales and influencing expectations about the market shares of future stocks of the competing formats.

Weak Lock-In

Alternatively, it is possible that a company might produce a product that is superior to the incumbent but is not sufficiently superior to cover the self-compatibility costs of switching to a new and different product. An example might be if a competitor produced, at an identical cost, a Zip-type drive in an incompatible system with a minor improvement in capacity, say from 250 MB to 260 MB. Current Zip consumers are not likely to switch to the new system since the very small advantage of the new system is unlikely to make it economical to throw out the old Zip drives and disks for the new alternative.

These consumers of Zip drives can be thought of as *weakly locked in* to the Zip system.[16] In this latter case it is inefficient for current consumers to switch to the new product, and although the term "lock-in" can be and has been used to describe this situation, it is quite distinct from the strong form of lock-in. If the incumbent already dominates a mature market, then the incumbent will remain the dominant technology, and it is efficient for it to remain the dominant technology. There is no necessity for there to be network effects or coordination problems in order to have weak forms of lock-in.

There are many, many instances of weak lock-in. You are unwilling to purchase a new computer merely three months after buying your current one even though new ones are slightly better. You continue driving your no longer brand-new car. You continue to live in a five-bedroom house after the kids have grown up and left, and the rooms largely sit empty. You continue to part your hair on the left. All of these, and millions of others, are examples of weak lock-in. All of these examples provide some limited protection to incumbents.

Weak lock-in has nothing to do with network effects or economies of scale. Weak lock-in shouldn't require new business strategies since it has been around for so long that old business strategies should have taken it into account. Business strategies that neglected switching costs would be derelict strategies, and perhaps the current literature can have some salutary impact in that dimension. But weak lock-in has little to do with moving to an information economy unless we think that learning to use digital products is more difficult than learning to use old pen-and-paper systems.

The final difference between the two forms of lock-in is that it is efficient for the economy to stay with the incumbent while the incumbent is weakly locked in. The costs of learning a new system are real costs, and if the new product is not sufficiently better to outweigh those costs, then it is efficient for society to stick with the old. Strong lock-in, on the other hand, causes inefficiency. If we could get all the users to switch to the new product, they would all be better off even after the costs of switching are included.

Impacts of Lock-In on First-Mover-Wins

Proponents of the strong form of lock-in essentially assume that, even if consumers wanted to switch to a better product, their fear that others might remain with the old product constrains them to remain with the old product. The challenger not only has to produce a better product that can overcome self-compatibility, but it also needs to overcome the consumer's cost of being incompatible with almost everyone else since it is assumed that no one else switches.[17] Critics of strong lock-in, on the other hand, believe that the expected market shares will depend mainly on self-compatibility. In other words, if the new product is sufficiently better than the old product that it pays individuals to switch (ignoring network effects), then the expectations of consumers will be such that they will expect other consumers to switch for the same reasons that they would want to switch. The new, superior product is thus able to dominate the market.

If the strong form of lock-in were to hold, the object lesson for companies would be to get to market first and largely ignore relative quality since even a significantly better product would not allow the challenger to dislodge the incumbent. This would be the claim of Brian Arthur and his followers.

The weak form of lock-in, on the other hand, gives little support for this tactic. The weak form of lock-in implies that the key to winning is to produce a product sufficiently better that it can overcome consumers' switching costs. Unless self-compatibility costs are very large, which is, to some extent, under the control of the challenger's product design, a better product will likely be able to overcome weak forms of lock-in. Emerson's dictum to build a better mousetrap would still work in the sense that a better mousetrap is understood to be one that is sufficiently better that it will overcome the costs of self-compatibility. While it is possible that self-compatibility costs could be so strong that the original seller would retain all customers because no improvements to the product could be made by competitors that could overcome self-compatibility costs, this result, besides being perfectly efficient, lacks novelty and seems unlikely. It would hardly provide a sufficient basis for a claim that, in the new information-based economy, rushing to market will suddenly be a winning strategy whereas it wasn't in the past. The weak form of lock-in has been around forever. It can be found in the most mundane activities.

I am used to going to a particular gas station. It is a habit. Even if the station across the street is a penny or two lower, I will continue going to the station at which I am comfortable. That makes it a weak form of lock-in. Does that mean that competing gas stations, in order to get my business, have to lower their prices by one-half to two-thirds, a number that has been put forward as the percentage differential required to break out of lock-in?[18] Obviously not. Although the precise number will differ by driver, surely a very large majority of drivers would pick the gas station charging $1.00 a gallon, or even $1.35, compared to their old gas station charging $1.50 a gallon. It is difficult to imagine anyone going to their old station and paying $1.50 when a nearby station is charging ninety cents a gallon.

Weak lock-in therefore seems an unlikely candidate to support first-mover-wins strategies.

What Does the Real World Tell Us About Strong Lock-In?

The concept of first-mover-wins, if it is to be indicative of something new, of something central to the information economy, requires a strong form of lock-in. Yet, there is no evidence that strong-form lock-in actually occurs. That explains why Altair, VisiCalc, and Ampex—the first companies to produce PCs, spreadsheets, and VCRs, respectively—are not today the leaders in those markets. Neither are any of the other early leaders in these markets still entrenched.

This is not to say that the advocates of a strong form of lock-in have not claimed support for it using real-world cases. Paul David, Brian Arthur, and their students have put forward various claims of actual instances of strong-form lock-in.

The two most popular examples of truly pernicious strong-form lock-in are the typewriter keyboard and the VCR.[19] These examples are popular in the press and particularly among academic authors. They are popular because they provide verisimilitude to what might otherwise appear as purely theoretical abstractions about the world. The problem is that these stories are counterfeits.

My research with Stephen Margolis, which formed the subject of my book with him, found no support for these claims of strong lock-in. This severely weakens support for the first-mover-wins hypothesis. Additionally, our examination of software markets found the evidence to be in direct contradiction of the first-mover-wins concept.

The keyboard story is described at great length elsewhere.[20] The basic story was first introduced to economists by Paul David and was later repeated numerous times, as for example in Shapiro and Varian's *Information Rules*. The story starts with the claim that, to prevent jamming of the mechanical keys, the typewriter mechanics who worked on the original QWERTY machine in the late 1800s came up with a design to slow down typing. Interestingly, not a shred of real evidence has been brought forward to support this claim. Rather, it appears that, to prevent jamming, the keyboard designers, through experimentation, came up with a way to shift the typing of successive letters from the left hand to the right. It also turns out that shifting successive letters between alternate hands leads to faster typing speeds.

In the 1930s, August Dvorak, a professor of ergonomics at the University of Washington, patented his own keyboard, which was painstakingly created from a systematic examination of which letters and pairs of letter were most commonly used in English writing and the subsequent application of this knowledge to position the keys to minimize the distance the fingers traveled. Dvorak's own research claimed that this keyboard design worked much better than the QWERTY design.

A study conducted by a component of the U.S. Navy during World War II purportedly demonstrated that Professor Dvorak's design was indeed 40 percent faster than the QWERTY design. If one examines the Navy study, as was not done by academic proponents of lock-in theory,[21] one discovers several important irregularities in its conduct that biased the results in favor of the Dvorak keyboard and that make it unacceptable as a "scientific" study.[22]

A more important problem with the claims of QWERTY's inferiority is that QWERTY detractors failed to discuss the most important study comparing the two keyboards. Professor Earl Strong from Penn State conducted a study in the 1950s for the General Services Administration (GSA). His experiment and its results received a great deal of publicity, including several articles in leading newspapers such as the *New York Times*.[23] Strong found that Dvorak was not superior to QWERTY. He also reported that the study conducted by the Navy during World War II was conducted by the Navy's chief expert in such matters, Lieutenant Commander August Dvorak, a fact that at least makes one suspicious of the impartiality of the Navy study.

Amazingly, this GSA study, which was far more readily available in most academic libraries than the Navy study, was entirely neglected by the advocates of strong-form lock-in. This is surprising, since Paul David, the popularizer of the story among economists, was a former president of the American Economic History Association and might have been expected to have gotten the history correct. In fact, there were some criticisms of Strong's study in the literature, but since the lock-in advocates never examined the GSA study, they weren't likely to find criticisms of that study. These criticisms of the GSA study, performed largely by supporters of Dvorak, do not seem terribly compelling, and the consensus in that literature appears to be that there is little difference in performance between the two keyboard designs.[24]

It is also the case that modern ergonomic studies of the keyboard and other experiments examining the costs of retraining typists to use the Dvorak keyboard are consistent with the GSA results and inconsistent with those reported by the Navy study.

This more complete history of the keyboards has been available to economists since 1990 but is almost never reported when lock-in advocates tell their version of the keyboard story. Instead, if they present any evidence contrary to the lock-in story, they usually bury it in a footnote, as Shapiro and Varian did, stating that there appears to be some disagreement in the academic literature.[25] The intent clearly seems to be to leave the reader with the impression that the keyboard lock-in story is correct even though there has never been an academic presentation refuting the facts that we uncovered.[26]

The VHS/Beta story, as an example of lock-in, or first-mover-wins, is even more flawed. [27] First, it is important to note that the Beta format was first on the scene and had a head start of about a year-and-a-half. It might be natural to ask where its first-mover advantage was since it was soon routed from this market by its competitor, VHS. The proponents of lock-in report, with some justification, that the videocassette recorder market wasn't yet very mature, and that the number of units sold was too small to give much of an advantage to Beta. But even more important, and perhaps the reason the videocassette recorder market didn't mature more rapidly under Sony's initial tutelage, was the fact that the initial Betamax could only record for one hour, eliminating the possibility of watching or recording movies on a single tape.

VHS had a larger cassette but otherwise had virtually the same technology as Betamax. The companies behind the two formats (Sony and Matsushita) had a patent-sharing agreement since they had jointly produced a prior-generation videocassette recorder. When Sony engineers saw the VHS machine, they thought it was a clone of the Betamax, so similar was it in terms of technology. VHS's much bigger tape allowed a longer playing time for a given quality of picture. It was the inferior playing time that led to the demise of the Betamax, not the fact that it was first or second or third.[28]

Now you might expect that this strong form of lock-in, given its impact on current thinking (not just business strategy but antitrust prosecutions such as the Microsoft case) must depend on more than just these two quite feeble stories. And it does, but not much more. It survives mostly due to the popularity of the economic theory that demonstrates that it could happen, on a few other slightly more far-fetched examples, and on the hopes and wishes of those who put forward the theory in the first place.[29]

So the claim has been made, by Brian Arthur and others, that the internal combustion engine was possibly a mistake that locked out superior alternatives such as the steam or electric engine.[30] If this seems pretty far-fetched, it's because it *is* far-fetched—but not too far-fetched to avoid serious academic scrutiny, particularly by those hoping to find a strong form of lock-in.[31] But even with every incentive to conclude that the internal combustion engine was a terrible mistake, that research could not come to such a conclusion.

There are other possibilities that have been suggested. Perhaps AM stereo should have replaced FM. Perhaps DC should have replaced AC as the standard for electrical generation. Perhaps quadraphonic sound of the 1980s should have replaced stereo. Perhaps the Macintosh operating system should have re-placed DOS (a graphical operating system did, but it happened to be called Windows). Perhaps railroads used the wrong gauge of tracks for the trains to run on.[32] These are all examples of possible instances of strong-form lock-in. These examples have also failed to make the case that their advocates were hoping to make.

There are as yet no real examples of strong-form lock-in. Someday, one or two might be found. But those will tend to be the exceptions that prove the rule.

Arthur and David have recently tried to turn the debate around by claiming that it is not they who should have to find strong forms of lock-in, but that the critics of strong-form lock-in should have to prove that every market has the most efficient product.[33] Arthur has said in several interviews that we (Liebowitz and Margolis) have not proved that QWERTY is the best possible keyboard.[34] Indeed, we have never made any such claim. Even if other keyboards were equally good or slightly better (which is what we actually concluded), that would not support claims of strong-form lock-in.

It is hard to provide better evidence of the difficulty of demon-strating strong-form lock-in than the current claim by its propo-nents that it is not their scientific responsibility to actually find any examples.[35] This claim began to surface two or three years ago. If they believe this current claim, one wonders about the pur-pose of their numerous attempts to find such examples during the previous fifteen years. Why were they bothering? Still, I don't want to sidetrack readers in what is largely an academic dispute that has gotten a bit out of hand.

In the lengthy examination of software markets that I con-ducted with Margolis, the only study of its kind that I know of, we found over and over again that the product that wins also happens to be as good as or better than the others. Even though these mar-kets appeared to be winner-take-all, having both network effects and economies of scale, and even though the leaders had very large market shares consistent with winner-take-all, good products pushed out lesser ones independent of which product was there first. VisiCalc, the first spreadsheet, was supplanted by the superior 1-2-3, only to be replaced by the superior Excel. Managing Your Money was supplanted by Quicken, and so forth.[36] This was true for markets where Microsoft was a player and in markets where it was not. It was true for Macintosh markets as well as Windows markets.

The Internet and First-Mover-Wins

For the most part, online retailing will not have the characteristics of winner-take-all or first-mover-wins. Most online retailers will not exhibit characteristics of network effects or instant scalability. Economies of scale, on the other hand, could be important, but there is little reason to think that bricks-and-mortar companies in the same industry would not possess equivalent economies of scale.

Take the case of Amazon, the company most famous for its strategy of forgoing current profits in order to establish its brand name and generate a large market share, a company willing to lose almost fifty cents for each dollar of sales in the name of market share growth. Was this a smart move? Does online bookselling exhibit the economic characteristics that will lead to winner-take-all or first-mover-wins?

As already mentioned, the creation of a Web site is a fixed cost perhaps imposing some economy-of-scale effects since the average cost of creating a Web site falls as output increases. But other costs of doing business on the Web are likely to swamp the cost of the initial creation of the Web site. Therefore, the fixed-cost component will be too small to dominate Amazon's overall average costs.

Network effects for Amazon are also very limited—things like product reviews by users and purchase circle information, but little else. Product reviews have network effect characteristics because the number of product reviews depends on the number of other users, and these reviews increase the value of the site to end-users. But product reviews, although likely to be of modest value to most users, are not likely to be sufficient to turn a market into winner-take-all. Barnes & Noble.com, whose Web site has far fewer reviews, never seemed to understand the potential importance of these network effects since it could have prodded consumers to provide more reviews by, for example, offering discount coupons to consumers who wrote reviews or contracting with an organization like *Book Review Digest* to provide its already published summary of major reviews. Either way, the network effects are almost certainly too small to lead to strong-form lock-in. Any lock-in that might occur here is almost certainly the weak form—familiarity with the site and pure habit. Also, Amazon did provide high-quality service and low prices, so there is little reason for users to switch. Barnes and Noble would need to either provide lower prices or higher quality if it wanted consumers to defect.

Amazon's winner-take-all characteristics, therefore, will be largely limited to those enjoyed by bricks-and-mortar booksellers. If bricks-and-mortar bookselling is not winner-take-all (and for all the bookstore agglomeration that has occurred in recent years, Barnes and Noble and Borders each hold only about 10 percent of the book retailing market), then online bookselling is also unlikely to be winner-take-all. Amazon's generation of enormous losses may have been largely without purpose except to create brand-name recognition and provide a quality experience for consumers, worthwhile goals but hardly ones that should require such enormous losses to achieve.

Additional Evidence

In 1999 I conducted a study for McKinsey trying to determine what causes companies to be successful. I looked at twenty different markets ranging from high-tech, such as Web portals, to low-tech, such as athletic apparel and discount retailers. The results were very interesting and quite consistent with those found in software markets as reported above.

There was a very strong relationship between those companies producing the best quality product and those companies that were most successful, measured by either above-normal profit, large market shares, or high stock market returns. Since PC manufacturers, software producers, and Web-site portals were all included in the study, they provide some specific cases to support the conclusion that building the better mousetrap is an essential ingredient for success, even in high-tech markets.

For example, in personal computer production, being first didn't count for much. Dell Computer Corporation, for example, wasn't the first seller of PCs, not by a long shot. IBM, Tandy, Kaypro, and many others (some long forgotten), were all to market earlier. What Dell has achieved for a long period of time is to have better performing products needing fewer repairs. Packard Bell, on the other hand, gained a large market share with low prices, emerging as the largest brand among home computer users in the early 1990s. Packard Bell was plagued with poor quality and service, however, and was going bankrupt as it was being bought by NEC in the late 1990s.[37]

Figure 3.1 indicates the reliability and service of four computer producers that were chosen for the McKinsey study. Dell, represented by the line with the embedded triangles, can be seen to be far above the industry norm, which was set at zero. Packard Bell, on the other hand, is seen to be far below the norm.[38]

Figure 3.2 reports on "bang for the buck" that vendors of PCs earned in various reviews. This is a measure of comparing the performance of the machine to the price of the machine. Again, Dell is far above the norm for the industry whereas Packard Bell, in the few reviews that Packard Bell allowed, did very badly.[39]

Similarly, Yahoo may have been one of the first search engines/portals, but more significantly, it was a higher quality portal than its competitors. This can be seen in figure 3.3. Again, the average score for all portals is set to zero, and it is obvious that

Figure 3.1. Reliability and Service for PCs

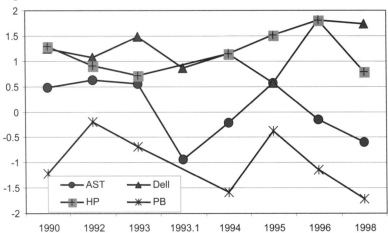

Figure 3.2. PC "Bang for buck"

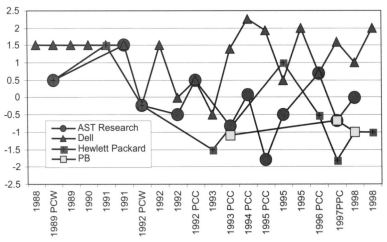

Figure 3.3. Quality of Search Engine/Portals

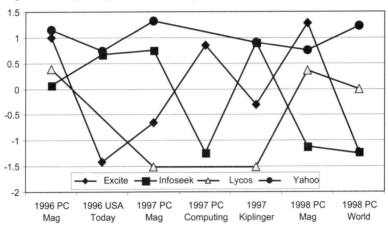

Yahoo is at the head of its class in terms of quality. That appears to be the reason it was successful and is probably the reason that it was one of the few Web portals able to achieve profitability.

Similarly, AOL was not the first online service. Prodigy, CompuServe, Genie, and others all preceded it. Yet AOL had the highest rankings in terms of quality, as can be seen in figure 3.4.

Prodigy, an early entrant with low initial prices, received terri-

Figure 3.4. Online Service Ratings

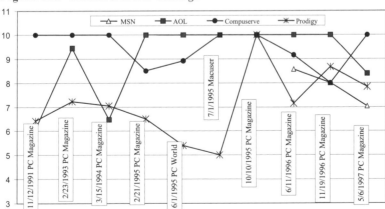

ble reviews, and when its prices rose to match those of its rivals, its market share eroded and the service became a weak also-ran. While AOL was becoming dominant, it was the most highly rated Internet service.

Again, the conclusion is consistent across many different high-tech markets: being early does not portend success if there are rivals with superior products. These findings are also consistent with recent evidence presented in the marketing literature.[40]

Business Lessons

This chapter has covered a great deal of material, including a peek behind the curtains of several academic disputes. The concept of lock-in, which has proved very appealing to business strategists, particularly those strategists of an academic stripe, was seen to be more subtle than has generally been understood. The type of lock-in that most strongly supports claims of first-mover advantages was seen to have no empirical support whatsoever. It appears to be a theory with little or no application to the world.

A company that takes big losses this year in order to win the market share wars is likely to find that it has won only a Pyrrhic victory. Businesses that still adhere to this notion and invest enormous sums for early advantage are likely to fail in the market. Much of the recent melt-down in high-tech sectors of the economy can be blamed on these misguided ideas.

That does not mean, however, that the concept of winner-take-all is discredited. There is a good deal of evidence that high-tech markets do incubate conditions that lead to very large market shares for the companies that are most successful in these markets. A company with a dominant market position, however, can expect to maintain that position only as long as consumers regard its products as the best.

But it needs to be understood that many, and perhaps most, Internet markets are no more likely to be winner-take-all than the bricks-and-mortar counterparts of these companies. For many industries, the Internet will offer an enhancement to business, but it will not bring about a fundamental restructuring of the business model. Just doing business on the Internet does not create the conditions for winner-take-all results. This was, and still is, a common misconception among the Internet cognoscenti.

Finally, what is probably the leading strategy for Internet companies is the same as the leading strategy for bricks-and-mortar companies: produce better products at lower costs. This strategy has worked numerous times, both in low-tech and high-tech industries, and it is not easy for competitors to copy successfully since talking quality is much easier than producing quality.

If you are faced with the choice of either rushing a weak product or Web site to market in order to be first or taking the necessary time to be best, go with best. Similarly, a late start in a market is not an insurmountable obstacle. Good Web businesses that continue to innovate may hold their positions for a long time, but you can't sit back in the expectation of milking those poor locked-in customers. That type of lock-in doesn't exist.

Notes

1. Morgan Stanley, "The Internet Retailing Report," May 28, 1997, p. 3.1. Internet, Mary Meeker; Retail, Sharon Pearson. This thinking was repeated in the June 1999 slide show, page 63, with a bullet point "First Mover Advantage Is Key—Whoever Signs Up the Buyers and Suppliers First Will Have Good Potential to Keep Them," at *http://morganstanley.com/techresearch/netcomhdbook/ih6.pdf.*

2. George Mannes, "First-Mover Advantage: What's It Really Worth?" The Street.com 1/26/99 7:00 AM ET. *http://www.thestreet.com/tech/internet/682198.html.*

3. There is literature attacking the first-mover doctrine, wishing to replace it with the second-mover or third-mover doctrine. See, for example, David Freedman, "Last Guys Finish First," *eCompany Now,* May 2001, available at *http://www.ecompany.com/articles/mag/0,1640,11229,FF.html.*

4. Jim, Carlton, "Dot-Com Boom Gives Builder Bechtel a Lift," *Wall Street Journal*, March 1, 2000, p. B1.

5. David Freedman, "Last Guys Finish First," referenced in note 3 above. But do not think that Freedman doesn't buy most of the lock-in story because he basically does. He reports that second or third mover may be the important starting position instead of just the first mover.

6. Carl Shapiro and Hal R.Varian, *Information Rules : A Strategic Guide to the Network Economy* (Boston: Harvard Business School Press, 1998), p. 169.

7. Kevin Kelly, *New Rules for the New Economy* (New York: Viking, 1998), p. 58.

8. Kelly, p. 60.

9. Arthur has been the subject of adoring stories in *Fortune* (James Aley and Lenore Schiff, "The Theory That Made Microsoft: It's Called 'Increasing Returns,' And It's One of the Hottest and Most Important Ideas in Economics Today," April 29, 1996, p. 65), the *New Yorker* ("The Force of an Idea," January 12, 1998), the *New York Times Magazine* (Peter Passell, "Why the Best Doesn't Always Win," May 5, 1996), the *Boston Globe* (David Warsh, "Sitting Alone at His Table by the Bar," July 3, 1994, Business section, p. 65), Britain's *Observer* (Ed Vulliamy, "Arthur's Big Idea: The Prophet of Profit; In the Hi-Tech Future, Punters Like Bill Gates Are Poised to Win the Whole Casino," March 8, 1998, p. 17), and a chapter in Mitchell Waldrop's book (*Complexity,* New York, Touchstone Books, 1992). In addition, he has had interviews with *Wired Magazine,* Booze-Allen & Hamilton's *Strategy & Business* magazine, and a somewhat more difficult interview in *PreText Magazine.*

10. Joel Kurtzman, interview with Brian Arthur by, Booze-Allen & Hamilton, *Strategy + Business,* second quarter 1998. *http://www. strategy-business.com/media/pdf/98209.pdf.*

11. There is an interesting debate about the novelty of the ideas that Arthur put forward and the putative intolerance of the economics profession to his ideas. See Paul Krugman "The Legend of Arthur: A Tale of Gullibility at *The New Yorker*," *Slate*, January 14, 1998 (*http://slate.msn.com/Dismal/98-01-14/Dismal.asp*). There were several interesting responses, including one from John Cassidy, the author of the flattering *New Yorker* piece about Arthur that stuck in Krugman's craw, and another from Mitchell Waldrop, the author of *Complexity* (*http://slate.msn.com/Features/Krugman/Krugman.asp*).

12. Shapiro and Varian certainly do not claim that traditional economics does not hold. In fact, they claim quite the opposite—that traditional economics with a few high-tech tweaks, such as network effects and lock-in, works just fine in explaining these markets. The problem was that they were willing to add to the economic toolbox concepts that had not been proven to exist in the economy.

13. There are numerous inconsistent definitions of lock-in that can be found in the economics literature. Liebowitz and Margolis ("Path Dependence, Lock-in, and History," *Journal of Law, Economics and Organization*, vol. 11, no. 1, (April 1995): 205–226) attempt to put some order to this chaos by defining three different types of path dependence or lock-in. Here I have simplified it down to two types where the information possessed by consumers about the future is complete. In the terminology of Liebowitz and Margolis, these two types reflect first-degree (weak) and third-degree (strong) path dependence.

14. Economies of scale differ in that once the product is purchased, the existence of economies of scale is irrelevant, which would not be true for network effects. This distinction, however, is not crucial.

15. There is a debate about these topics in the economics literature. Participants include Paul David, Brian Arthur, Michael Katz, Carl Shapiro, Steve Margolis, myself, and many others. A more accessible version of one aspect of these debates, with proxies often standing in for the main players, can be found at the economic history discus-

sion groups: *http://eh.net/FORUMS/PathDepe.html* and *http:// eh.net/FORUMS/QWERTYSu2.html*. Some of the important academic articles on network effects in addition to those already mentioned, are: M. L. Katz and C. Shapiro, "Technology Adoption in the Presence of Network Externalities," *Journal of Political Economy* 94 (1986): 822–841; J. Farrell and G. Saloner, "Standardization, Compatibility, and Innovation," *Rand Journal* 16 (1985): 70–83; and S. J. Liebowitz and S. E. Margolis, "Path Dependence, Lock-In and History," *Journal of Law, Economics, and Organization* 11 (1995): 205–226 and "Are Network Externalities a New Source of Market Failure?" *Research in Law and Economics* 17 (1995): 1–22.

16. I am ignoring here the possibility that consumers might want to be compatible with each other. Since self-compatibility is sufficient to keep the old technology in place (assuming that the incumbent already controlled a majority of potential consumers), there is no alteration in the result that compatibility with others might bring.

17. See Brian Arthur's example of decision-making among consumers that can be found in "Competing Technologies, Increasing Returns, and Lock-In by Historical Events," *Economic Journal* 97 (1989): 116–131. His consumers are myopic and seem to live only for the moment since they do not look to the future at all.

18. Brian Arthur has claimed that a new product has to be 200–300 percent better to break the grip of lock-in. This number seems to be taken entirely out of thin air and really is based on the strong form of lock-in although he has never made any distinction between strong and weak forms of lock-in. See, for example, his article in the *Harvard Business Review* where he states: "A new product often needs to be twice or three times better in some dimension—price, speed, convenience—to dislodge a locked-in rival." W. B. Arthur, "Increasing Returns and the New World of Business," *Harvard Business Review* 74, no. 4 (July-August 1996):100. This can be found at *http://www.santafe.edu/arthur/Papers/Pdf_files/HBR.doc*.

19. Technically, these are formats and not products. The QWERTY keyboard patent expired before the market matured, but many, in fact

virtually all, rival keyboard manufacturers eventually adopted it. The VHS standard, on the other hand, was still owned when the format became dominant and the market large and mature.

20. For the original academic claim by economists see P. A. David, "Clio and the Economics of QWERTY," *American Economic Review* 75 (1985): 332–337. For the refutation of David's story, see S. J. Liebowitz, and S. E. Margolis, "The Fable of the Keys," *Journal of Law and Economics* 33 (1990):1–26, which is available at *http://wwwpub. utdallas.edu/~liebowit/keys1.html.*

21. David admitted to a *Wall Street Journal* reporter that he had never read the Navy study that he talked about in his article. See Lee Gomes, "Economists Decide to Challenge Facts of the QWERTY Story," *Wall Street Journal,* February 25, 1998.

22. This is discussed in Liebowitz and Margolis 1990, especially the text material in and around footnote 25.

23. See "U.S. Plans to Test New Typewriter," *New York Times*, November 1, 1955; "Revolution in the Office," *New York Times,* November 30 1955; "Key Changes Debated," *New York Times,* June 18, 1956; "U.S. Balks at Teaching Old Typists New Keys," *New York Times,* July 2, 1956; and Peter White, "Pyfgcrt vs. Qwertyuiop," *New York Times,* January 22, 1956.

24. See for example: H. Yamada, "A Historical Study of Typewriters and Typing Methods: From the Position of Planning Japanese Parallels," *Journal of Information Processing* 2 (1980): 175–202. Yamada has claimed that Strong was biased against Dvorak, a claim that is repeated by current advocates of the Dvorak keyboard.

25. For example, Shapiro and Varian (cited in note 6) present the QWERTY example on pages 185 and 186. After presenting Paul David's strong lock-in story as if it were true, they mention in the last sentence or two that something appears wrong with the story because computer keyboards are so easily reprogrammed that strong-form lock-in would seem impossible. Yet on page 233 they are

back to stating that QWERTY is an inferior design. They do try to cover themselves by citing in a footnote the Liebowitz and Margolis 1990 presentation of the typewriter history, but it appears to be more an example of covering themselves against claims that they missed a relevant article than attempting to present full information for their readers. For readers interested in other fables that economists and others like to claim are true see Dan Spulber's *Famous Fables of Economics* (Malden, MA: Basil Blackwell, 2002).

26. Paul David has been promising a rejoinder for about ten years now. Instead of just admitting that his original 1985 paper had grievous historical inaccuracies, he has tried to muddy the waters by writing papers on related but different topics. See, for example, Paul A. David, "Path Dependence and the Quest for Historical Economics: One More Chorus of the Ballad of QWERTY" (1997), available at *http://www.eh.net/Clio/Publications/pathnotes.html* in which he states: "Consequently, it is proper for me at the outset to caution those readers who are hopeful of finding herein some further technical details and narrative material on the evolution of typewriter keyboard layouts. Although they are going to be disappointed on that account, there will be another, more suitable place in which to consider my detailed rejoinders to the dubious factual allegations that have circulated concerning the 'true story' of QWERTY." He also states "The historical arguments and evidence offered to support that critique are reexamined in my forthcoming paper: 'Neoclassical economists at the keyboard: Is there a cure for "repetitive thought injuries?'" Four years later, this paper has yet to see the light of day, although David was apparently so proud of having thought up the title that he couldn't keep from referencing it as an upcoming paper.

27. See Liebowitz and Margolis, "Path Dependence, Lock-In, and History," 1995 in note 13 above for a more detailed version of this history (itself based on the book *Fast Forward*, by James Lardner, W.W. Norton, New York, 1987.) For a view that states that VHS won mainly because it had a superior coalition of companies, see M. A. Cusumano, Y. Mylonadis, and R. S. Rosenbloom, "Strategic Maneu-

vering and Mass-Market Dynamics—The Triumph of VHS Over Beta," *Business History Review* 66, no. 1 (Spring 1992): 51–94. There are several problems with their story, however. First, the number of companies likely to join a coalition is itself a function of the perceived likelihood of success of a product in the market. Second, Cusumano et al. pay too little attention to the inherent advantage of having a larger tape in allowing longer playing times and reasonable picture qualities. Analog recording of all types benefits from more tape passing the head in a given amount of time, a feature that benefited VHS and that was crucial in having RCA, the largest American seller of televisions, join the VHS camp. Third, in order for the number of producers to matter, either their additional brand names or their additional capacity must help. Yet, evidence from Cusumano et al indicates that the brand names of the various camps were fairly evenly split in the market shares for televisions. Sony had a strong brand name (and Zenith, the number two television producer in the United States, put its name on the Betamax, as did Sanyo and Toshiba). Cusumano et al., provide no evidence that there was a shortage of capacity in the Beta camp, even if their productive capacity was less than that of the VHS camp.

28. In fact, there were many previous videocassette recorder formats, all failures.

29. You might think that an economic theory becomes popular because it is very useful in explaining how the world works. While true on occasion, a theory may very well become popular when it is elegant and allows many academics to write something new, different, or exciting. Novelty sometimes appears to be more important than correctness, at least in the short run.

30. See W. Brian Arthur "Positive Feedbacks in the Economy," *Scientific American*, 262, (February 1990): 92–99.

31. See David Kirsch, "The Electric Car and the Burden of History: Automotive Systems Rivalry in America" (Ph.D. diss., Stanford University, 1996). I should note that Stanford is the home of Paul David, of

QWERTY fame (who was on the dissertation committee) and was also home to Brian Arthur when he was writing on these topics.

32. On this there is a dissertation and paper by VanVleck demonstrating that British railroad gauges were not a major mistake. See V. N. L. VanVleck "Delivering Coal by Road and Rail in Britain: The Efficiency of the 'Silly Little Bobtailed' Coal Wagons," *Journal of Economic History* 57, no. 1 (March 1997): 139–160.

33. See Paul David's paper "At Last, a Remedy for Chronic QWERTY Skepticism!" Prepared for presentation at the European Summer School in Industrial Dynamics (ESSID), held at l'Institute d'Études Scientifique de Cargese (Corse), France, September 5–12, 1999. This paper can be found at *http://www.eh.net/Publications/remedy.shtml.* Of special interest is the section titled "'Oompha-Metrics' and the Burden of Proof."

34. Here is the quote from the interview Arthur had with *PreText Magazine*: "As for the QWERTY keyboard, if Margolis and Liebowitz can prove it's the best, my hat is off to them." The interview can be found at *http://www.pretext.com/may98/columns/intview.htm.* He actually says much more, mainly in a rather ad hominem fashion. Here are a few nuggets: "As far as I can see, the Liebowitz and Margolis arguments are ideological arguments for the far right . . . I find I'm puzzled by all of this because it's a bit like debating evolution with creationists . . . Well, again, you only get excited about that if you belong to the right wing of American ideology." This probably is a nastier debate than most, but all the ad hominem attacks come from their ranks. Readers can determine for themselves why that might be.

35. For a discussion of these claims see Peter Lewin, "The Market Process and the Economics of QWERTY: Two Views" *Review of Austrian Economics,* 14, no. 1 (March 2001): 65–96, available at *http://www.utdallas.edu/~plewin/QWERTY%20condensed.pdf.*

36. See *Winners, Losers, & Microsoft,* especially chapters 7, 8, and 9.

37. See, for example, Peter Burrows and Irene Kunii, "Packard Bell NEC Hits the Restart Button," *Business Week* (June 28, 1999): 38.

38. These results are taken from data reported in *PC Magazine*. For full information see Stan Liebowitz, "Product Quality and the Economic Performance of Firms," report for McKinsey and Company, October 15, 1999, which is available at *http://wwwpub.utdallas.edu/~liebowit/mckinsey.pdf*.

39. PCW stands for *PC World*, PCC stands for *PC Computing*. Otherwise, if no acronym is given, the review is for *PC Magazine*. These magazines review computers sent to them by manufacturers but do not buy review machines. Manufacturers therefore need to actively send their machines in for review, something that Packard Bell rarely did, presumably because of the poor showings of their machines.

40. See Gerard Tellis and Peter Golder, *Will and Vision: How Latecomers Grow to Dominate Markets*, New York, McGraw-Hill, 2002.

Chapter 4

The (Non) Ubiquity of E-Tailing?

The retail markets that most lend themselves to Internet sales are those with items that (a) have high value relative to bulk, (b) are not "experience" goods, (c) are not instant gratification goods, and (d) are not perishable goods as defined and explained below.

At the height of the Internet craze, the received wisdom was that Internet retailing had advantages that were going to turn bricks-and-mortar companies into relics, as if from some prehistoric age. From one of our favorite pundits we have

> Creation of New Distribution Channels Create Opportunities for Retailers. The Internet represents the potential creation of the greatest, most efficient distribution vehicle in the history of the planet.[1]
>
> Mary Meeker and Mark Mahaney, Morgan Stanley

Of course, the Internet improves the transfer of information, not the distribution of physical commodities. But given the hyperbole of the time, this point was of little matter. Other commentators made similar statements.

> Economies and interest rates can come and go, but every business over the next few year must aggressively become an e-business. . . .
>
> Robert Austrian, Bank of America[2]

This is from an interview with Jeff Bezos, founder of Amazon

> *Business Week:* How will online selling change physical-world retailing?
>
> Bezos (Amazon Founder): The short answer is that strip malls go away because physical retailing is not going to be able to compete on price. That can't happen. If you study the economics, online retailing is just more efficient. Online stores are going to be the low-cost providers.
>
> As a result, that leaves other things for physical stores to compete on, and there are lots of dimensions that are important to customers besides price. One of them is entertainment. . . . A second category of things is when you need something right now, this minute. In that case, you need to do the last inch of delivery yourself. Which means you pop in the car and go to the store, and you are willing to pay that half an hour to do that. . . . So what's going to happen in my opinion is that stores are going to get more entertaining. The quality of the sales associates is going to go up to make that experience more pleasant. Stores are going to get cleaner. Every dimension you can imagine of making a physical store better is going to happen.[3]

So, we are to believe, Internet retailing is going to be so formidable a threat that bricks-and-mortar retailers are going to have to become veritable Ringling Brothers Circuses, with sales associates jumping through hoops, if the stores are to remain viable.

The last few years have seen numerous Internet companies formed to sell everything from airline tickets to dog food. Everything, it seemed, was going to be sold over the Internet. The opinions expressed in the above quotations were taken quite seriously. Now that these expectations have been deflated by the burst of the Internet bubble, what would be a more rational set of expectations?

How Might the Internet Transform Business?
E-Ordering vs. E-Retailing

It is important to distinguish between Internet-based sales, which alter the nature of the current distribution system, and the use of the Internet to replace the telephone as a means of ordering a product, but with distribution in the traditional sense. Ordering a pizza online instead of calling up the store with the telephone is hardly a major transformation of the pizza business. In each case a local storefront will be used to create the pizza and to serve as a location for delivery vehicles. A minor part of the transaction—the order—differs, but this is not a significant alteration in the pizza business.

There are several ways in which the Internet can alter a business model:

1. It can alter the shopping experience, replacing actual physical stores and merchandise with virtual stores and virtual merchandise.

2. It can alter the way the product is purchased after shopping has been completed.

3. It can alter the distribution (including warehousing and delivery) of the product, creating a distribution system to move the product from the manufacturer to the consumer.

A fully transforming business model makeover would include all three of these components. Several new e-businesses, such as Web-based grocery stores (examined below in the section entitled "Examples of Markets Likely to Resist the Internet Assault") have attempted these complete makeovers.

In other instances, partial makeovers are all that companies are likely to attempt. For example, many bricks-and-mortar companies allow some degree of shopping over the Net, often as a replacement for some sort of catalog or mail-order shopping that they had previously used. This type of activity combines (1) and (2) above.

If a company only provides information about the product but doesn't offer online purchase, the Web merely replaces advertising circulars. This is a minor change for most companies and one that would be unlikely to alter the industry in any serious way. The Internet just becomes one of several means by which the company tries to communicate with potential customers.

It is difficult to see traditional mail order surviving since the Internet would seem to dominate it on all fronts. Internet pages should be a less expensive technology for selling the product to consumers in comparison to the expense of printing and mailing circulars. Taking orders online should be faster and surer than using human operators. Since both methods use the same distribution methods, it seems there is no way for mail order to compensate for its deficiencies unless it turns out that many consumers never adopt the Web or that consumers prefer to look at physical pictures as opposed to pictures on the Web.

Characteristics of Products That Are Likely to Determine the Extent of the Internet Transformation

Consumers like to see and touch many of the items they buy. They are used to and tend to demand instant gratification. They also like to save money. They like to avoid lines. These are somewhat contradictory desires, and only some are better met by virtual retailing than by traditional bricks-and-mortar retailing.

Indisputably, the Internet does provide some advantages to consumers: a large selection, no lines at the register, and perhaps lower costs. Yet there are also many disadvantages. You cannot touch, smell, squeeze, shake, or feel products on the Internet. Transportation costs are likely to be higher, delivery less than immediate, and its current status as a sales-tax-free haven is likely to be short-lived. Also, some products are best sold with a hands-on demonstration, and a move to Internet sales could endanger the functioning of these markets.

Some products, such as airline tickets or financial instruments such as stocks, can easily move to the Web since there is no disadvantage to their being sold on the Web—no transportation costs, no examination required, no instant gratification. In these cases the Internet is the natural retail outlet. I expect that virtually all products such as software, music, videos, and other "digital" intellectual products will eventually be sold over the Web. Other products do not seem as well-suited to sale on the Internet. The next few sections discuss the factors that alter the likelihood of successful Internet transformations.

Size and Bulk Relative to Value

If we were to create a list of products based on the ratio of weight (bulk) to price, we would have a ranking of products that would tell us which were likely to be shipped over large distances and which were not. Some products, such as cement, are large and bulky, particularly relative to their value. At the other extreme are products like diamonds, which have very high value relative to bulk. Such a ranking would be a very good predictor of which products are produced and shipped over large distances to customers and which products tend to be produced near consumers with minimum shipping.

Cement, having a low value relative to its weight, will tend to be produced locally. That is because the cost of shipping it over large distances would fairly quickly overwhelm production costs, giving local manufacturers a large advantage over distant manufacturers. Diamonds, on the other hand, can be shipped large distances with the shipping cost comprising only a small percentage of price, and thus it is not surprising that diamonds *are* shipped great distances

Digitized, information-based products have the lowest ratio of weight to price for the simple reason that their weight is zero.

These products travel at enormous speeds on electronic networks such as the Internet. These products, in their raw form, must be delivered over a network, and the Internet is currently the king of the networks.

This is relevant to Internet commerce because products sold over the Internet have to be delivered to the consumer in some fashion. It does not make sense to use a full Internet model that tends to require shipping using FedEx or UPS to sell products that do poorly being shipped over large distances.

Of course, it is also important to realize that these products were delivered to consumers in some fashion before the Internet came into being. The relevant criterion, therefore, would be a comparison of the costs of delivering products sold over the Internet with the costs of delivering products by more traditional means.

Immediate Gratification Factor (Impulse Buying)

Supermarkets carry several types of items at the checkout counter: candy, magazines, and, of course, trashy tabloids. These are not randomly chosen items but instead represent products that retailers believe tend to be purchased on a whim and for immediate gratification. Although it is certainly possible to stock up on candy, for example, it is often the case that a consumer really just wants to purchase one piece to throw in his or her mouth. Indeed, the candy sold at the checkout counter is usually not a large package but an individual item instead.

For some consumers, the purchase of an automobile can be an impulse good, due perhaps to either great wealth or to some form of personality disorder, so that, in this case, impulse buying need not be an aspect of the product itself. Although I do not pretend to be able to quantify the extent of impulse purchases, there are undoubtedly many purchases that are made for immediate gratification.

With one important exception, it does not require any great effort to understand why these types of purchases are not going to

occur over the Internet—the delivery delay on the Internet eliminates the possibility of immediate gratification. Therefore, these
types of purchases will not migrate to the Internet.

Digital products are the important exception alluded to above.
Because digital products can be transmitted over the Internet (except, as I am often reminded, if the connection fails) the delay
between purchase and delight is actually greater when purchasing
the products in bricks-and-mortar stores, reversing the relative
gratification speeds of the two types of retailing. In this instance,
the Internet provides virtually immediate gratification, making it
the channel of choice for digital products purchased by impulse
buyers.

Perishability

Some products lose their useful attributes over short periods of
time. Most foods that are not vacuum-packed, particularly meats
and produce, can last for only a few days or weeks before they go
bad. Products with a shelf life of less than a few days are poor
candidates to be sold over the Internet when the purchase entails
shipment of the product to the final consumer. The exception
would be that small number of expensive food items that have
generally been sold through mail order. Some small number of
steaks, lobsters, desserts, and other food items have historically
been sold and shipped in packages containing dry ice to keep them
frozen during the delivery period. These are perishable foods with
a very high ratio of value/shipping cost that could just as well be
sold over the Internet. Clearly, it would be uneconomical to ship
most ordinary perishables in this manner, and the Internet does
nothing to change this equation.

Experience Products and Free-Riding

Some products require close examination before the consumer is
comfortable making a purchase. These are products that do not
have a high degree of uniformity or, perhaps, products that are
bought infrequently so that consumers cannot rely on learned in-

formation from their previous purchase since the products have since changed.

These are products like clothing where consumers find fitting rooms to be very important. Automobiles, for which the "drive" and looks are important, will tend to require close inspection. Audio speakers belong in this category because they are highly variable and depend on the tastes of the consumer, thus often requiring the consumer to listen to them before purchase.

Examples of products that do not require inspection are books, where each copy of a title is essentially identical to all other copies, aspirin, videotapes, rulers, and so forth.

There is an interesting issue that arises in the case of products that sell best with demonstrations. There is a problem known as "free-riding" that economists believe was responsible for efforts by some manufacturers to keep retailers from charging too low a price for their products.

Manufacturers should be very happy to have retailers selling their products for very low prices. Since retailers pay the same price to manufacturers no matter how little the retailers sell the product for, the manufacturer gets to sell a larger number of units without lowering the price received from the retailer. It seems that it would only increase the manufacturer's profits if the retailer sells the product at a very low price. Why manufacturers would want to prevent retailers from lowering prices then becomes a puzzle.

The basic paradox is solved by examining what would happen to manufacturers if some retailers tried to benefit from the demonstrations made by other retailers. Assume, for example, that some automobile dealers provided test drives and others did not. It is costly to provide test drives—someone from the dealership often has to accompany the potential consumer on the test drive, the cars get extra miles put on them, and so forth. A dealer that didn't provide such service would have lower costs and could therefore afford to sell his automobiles at lower prices than dealers that did provide this service. If consumers wanted test drives, they could go to the dealer that provided such drives and then, when they had determined which car they wanted to buy, they could go to the dealer with the lower price. The dealer with the low prices could even suggest this to consumers who ask for a demonstration. This would tend to have the impact of driving the dealers that provided test drives out of business. This is the free-riding alluded to above.[4]

The automobile manufacturer may well find that the end result—no demonstrations of automobiles—is not conducive to efficient sales of new vehicles. In the past, this has led to attempts by manufacturers to control the price set by retailers, restricting the ability of retailers to charge a lower price than the one charged by retailers who offer demonstrations—who need to charge a higher price in order to pay for those demonstrations. Once these price restrictions were in place, discounters couldn't benefit from free-riding since consumers would purchase the product from the dealer providing the demonstration. These restrictions on *minimum* price were put in place as state laws known as "fair trade laws" or "resale price maintenance." They were struck down by the courts and are no longer on the books.

As a consequence, manufacturers now try to restrict the outlets that can sell their goods to those they believe will provide sufficient services to consumers. An example of this behavior is Apple computer, which, during the 1980s and early 1990s, tried very hard to keeps its computers out of the hands of discounters, particularly the mail-order discounters who provided no presales services.

This same type of problem could arise with Internet retailing. Internet retailers might very well not provide the level of service that manufacturers consider necessary for the proper long-term sales of their product. In that case, manufacturers might fear that Internet retailers would be successful enough as competitors to prevent the full-service retailers from providing full service.

It would then be in the best interest of these manufacturers to keep their products away from Internet retailers. Therefore, even if the Internet allowed retailers of such products to become profitable by free-riding off their bricks-and-mortar counterparts, we would expect manufacturers of these types of products to fight to keep their products off the Internet.

Thin Markets

Thin markets are those that have few buyers (and usually few sellers) of a product because the product is just not very popular or perhaps not very affordable. Although not necessarily an intrinsic characteristic of the product itself, this is a characteristic of the market for the product. Products that are sold in thin markets are not good candidates for bricks-and-mortar retailers since bricks-and-mortar retailers tend to service a particular geographic area, and most local populations are likely to be too small to justify the fixed costs of a bricks-and-mortar retailer. Sometimes, large urban areas may be able to support a retailer of such products.

Being on the Internet eliminates geographic confines. Of course, this isn't much different from mail order, which also has no confining geographic region, although mail order is limited to the reach of its catalogs. The Internet is an ideal way to sell products that may have at one time been sold only in specialty shops in larger cities with sufficient population densities to support a bricks-and-mortar store. We might be talking about unusual herbs and spices, foreign "delicacies" that appeal to a very small number of palates, specialized books, tools, instruments, and so forth.

One problem with many of these products is that they are popular in their home country but often appeal to small constituencies in other countries. The Internet might allow sales to be made directly from the country of origin, bypassing the middleman specialty dealer.

The eBay site allows the trading of products that might otherwise have thin markets. By bringing many buyers and sellers to one location, and by providing good search tools, buyers and sellers of unusual commodities can interact with one another. The very large number of eBay customers tends to thicken what would under more normal circumstances be a thin market. Several years ago the *Wall Street Journal* ran a humorous story about the selling and buying of soiled panties on eBay; while the intent was humor, this clearly was a thin market that was able to benefit from the Internet's powers to aggregate across geographic boundaries.

The Role of Taxes

Taxes, or more specifically the lack of taxes, are important if we wish to understand and predict the size and scope of Internet retailing. Currently, the Internet has benefited from its status as a tax-free haven for out-of-state consumers, who save about 7 percent relative to bricks-and-mortar purchases. This is a substantial savings and would be expected to significantly increase Internet sales.

Notwithstanding the contrary claims of politicians, governments are loath to exempt significant economic activities from taxes. It is the height of naïveté to think otherwise. Further, bricks-and-mortar retailers can legitimately claim that they are being unfairly penalized in their competition with online retailers since they are at a price disadvantage brought about by the tax inequity. It is not clear why an industry, whether nascent or mature, needs tax protection. If the industry provides value, it will survive, with or without tax advantages. If it cannot survive without tax advantages, that is a clear signal that it should not survive.

It therefore seems very likely that, if the Internet becomes an important retailing force, this tax-free status will come to an end. When it does, sales on the Internet will be smaller than their current trajectory would indicate.

The five-year moratorium on taxes that had existed until late 2001 was recently renewed for two more years. Still, states have been working to simplify their tax codes to meet the Supreme Court's objection to taxing mail-order companies, an objection based on the crazy quilt of retail tax policies that existed in many localities and that would be very costly for companies outside the locality to keep track of.

Congress could very well eventually allow states to tax Internet commerce along with other forms of mail order. If mail-order and Internet sales continue to carve out larger pieces of the retail pie, we can expect that a sales tax on these activities will eventually be put in place.

An article in CNET news quotes Paul Misener, Amazon's vice president in charge of global public policy, as stating "Our model is not predicated on the non-collection of these taxes . . . I like to say that if true simplification occurs, companies will be able to handle it, address it and observe it."[5] It may well be that their business model is not predicated on avoiding these taxes, but it would be extremely naïve to believe that a new 7 percent payment that goes into government coffers would not have a significant negative impact on Internet sales.

What Types of Products Are Most Compatible with Full-Fledged E-Tailing?

There are hundreds of thousands of retail products, any one of which could, in principle, be sold over the Internet. The characteristics described above provide guidance in trying to understand which of them might do better than others.

Digitized Products

Products that are inherently digital are obviously the most natural candidates for transmission over the Internet. Computer programs, which have always been digital, can be stored on various media and delivered that way but are most conveniently and rapidly delivered over the Internet. Therefore, it would be natural to expect that this would be the primary form of delivery for these types of products. This implies that, in the future, retailers like CompUSA should expect to have to increase the space devoted to hardware relative to the shrinking space that they should be devoting to software.

Of greater interest are products that used to be delivered in some analog fashion but which are now capable of being delivered digitally. These include sound recordings, television, radio, movies, and other pure-information products.

We need to distinguish here between the digital property and its physical manifestation. Virtually any intellectual product, be it a song, poem, movie, or painting, can be digitized. Once cast in electronic form, however, it needs to be transformed into a physical entity that then allows the contents to be released in some way so users can enjoy its characteristics, since we cannot consume electrons directly. Music, for example, when digitized, most often needs to be transformed into some physical manifestation, such as a CD or a cassette, before one can listen to it. Many consumers have the equipment to create CDs or cassettes from digital formats such as MP3. What is new, however, is that the most popular digital format, MP3, has created a market for devices that specialize in playing back music digitized in this format. This is a new form of physical manifestation based on a digital standard that may some day become the dominant physical standard in which music is stored for use, although the record companies will do everything in their power to prevent it from being so.

Movies can now be stored digitally in one of several physical manifestations with DVDs in the MPEG format being the most modern. Currently, the only individuals who can benefit from downloadable movies are those who use their computers to play movies since there are very few consumer DVD-writing machines available that might allow a user to download a movie and transfer the information to a disc that could then be viewed on the television with a DVD player. Most consumers still store movies in analog formats using the VHS standard, but this is changing since sales of DVDs have been rapidly increasing. DVDs appear likely to diffuse through the economy the same way CD players did so that they may overtake VHS machines in just a few years. When that happens (and when DVD-writers become common), downloading movies from the Internet will almost certainly be the more efficient system of delivery and will replace the current videotape rental system, if piracy issues can be resolved and if enough consumers get truly fast Internet links.

Books and magazines can also be delivered digitally although it is not yet clear that the physical manifestations of these digital products will be acceptable substitutes for our current printed-paper-based products. It is still an open question whether and when electronic devices that display the words from magazines and books will be considered the equal of commercially-printed paper, which is currently the physical manifestation of choice for books and magazines. The portability of paper and the quality of the print displayed on the page still seem, for most people, to out-weigh any advantages of electronic devices, such as the ability to store multiple books, do word searches, or read in the dark. How-ever, paper's current advantages are likely to be eliminated by the continuous tide of progress that sweeps away old technologies and replaces them with new ones.

There is no reason that these products will not all move to the Internet eventually because the Internet will provide the most immediate delivery, the least costly delivery, and the most in-formed delivery. It is difficult to imagine that bricks-and-mortar alternatives will continue to exist except to the extent that the Internet fails to penetrate the population of consumers. We are likely to see it first with computer programs and music since these have been digitized for a long time. This digitization, of course, opens up the whole issue of piracy and copyright, a subject I dis-cuss in detail in chapter 7.

Information

A somewhat different form of information transmittal consists of items such as airline, car, and hotel reservations, stock purchases, news retrieval, classified advertising, and so forth. All of these are a form of information and, as such, lend themselves to an easy form of digitization. The Internet should be able to allow informa-tion to be transmitted more economically, more rapidly, and more efficiently than the telephone or the mail. In order for this to happen, however, the Internet needs to be able to provide the same level of information that a skilled operator could provide. That means that the Web site needs to be easy enough to navigate that novices can find what they are looking for easily and quickly. It also means that the information that is provided needs to be as flexible and detailed as that made available by a live person. This is no easy task.

For example, if you try to book a hotel room on Microsoft's Expedia Web site, you can often get the price, but you may or may not be told what type of bed is available. You may be told that the price is for a "standard room" without a definition of what a "standard room" is. To make matters worse, the confirmation code that you often get is an Expedia confirmation, not a hotel confirmation. I often find myself calling up the hotel to make sure that the booking went through properly and that I am getting the type of room I want. I also usually double-check that my credit card actually holds the room for late arrival since the Web site is sometimes unclear about that.

Yet Expedia is probably one of the better reservation sites. A Web site is run by a computer, and to be able to emulate what a human operator can do, it needs to be set up with great care. Only when Web sites reach this level of sophistication can we expect the Web to replace the phone for almost any kind of reservation.

To the extent that investors do not rely on brokers for information but only for placing trades, using the Internet to track stocks and place orders should provide a better alternative. Again, this assumes that the Web site works. And of course, once computers are taught to bend the truth, they can replace salesmen of all sorts.

One potential problem was exposed during some of the more volatile heavy-trading days. Some of the servers for discount brokers were overwhelmed and it became very difficult, if not impossible, to have trades executed online. The online brokers all promised to fix the problem, and it is certainly the case that an old-fashioned telephone-based system could equally well suffer from this sort of peak-load problem.

Again, the Web sites need to be capable of doing their job properly. TD Waterhouse, one of the brokers I use, has a fairly nice site. But if you try to buy options, you need to get the option symbols somewhere else. Options have complicated symbols based on the strike price and expiry date. One might think that brokers would have the sense to just ask you for the underlying stock, the strike price, and the expiry date, and then provide you with the symbol (as did another broker of mine who was then bought out by Waterhouse). But Waterhouse expected the customer to know these things. This is the type of oversight that needs to be corrected if we expect machines to replace humans in these activities. Eventually, these inconveniences will be corrected, or else those sites that fail to provide such information will be driven out of business by those that are better able to provide this information.

Classified advertising is one area where the Internet should shine. There are strong network effects in the listing of used and often hard-to-find items. Sellers write the descriptions, so there is little expertise required from others. It is hard to imagine that most classified advertising will not move to the Internet. This will be discussed in more detail below.

Books and CDs

Although I have just described how books can be digitized and might therefore be sold directly over the Internet, this is not going to be the primary form of distribution for some time to come. Until that time arrives, traditional paper books will represent the vast majority of book sales. Books play a particularly important role in the history of e-retailing since the most famous e-retailer—Amazon—began by selling books online. Jeff Bezos, the founder of Amazon, likes to tell the story that, after realizing the potential of the Internet, he thought about various products that might best be sold over the Internet and came up with books. Was he right?

Based on the characteristics that are compatible with Internet sales, it would appear that he made a wise choice. Books are not perishable. Every copy is virtually the same as every other copy so there is no need to examine the product for defects. The content of books is not, at least for most readers, an experience good. To the extent that it is, Amazon has done a good job of providing, or at least trying to provide, the level of experience that could be achieved by potential consumers in a bricks-and-mortar store by offering reviews and often an introductory chapter to give the consumer a feel for the content of the book. This may actually be preferable to standing in a bookstore and reading a book for fifteen or twenty minutes to get a feel for the content. Further, the few days' wait imposed by the Internet is not likely to be of great concern to most consumers. Virtually the same factors are at work in the CD market, making that another good candidate for Internet sales—until, that is, the digital code is sold directly online.

The final factor in evaluating the concept of selling books over the Internet is the shipping cost. Here we have an open question of whether the Internet provides sufficient value. The Internet retailer replaces the shipping cost of the bricks-and-mortar seller and the consumer's cost in driving to his store with the external shipping cost of an outside vendor such as UPS or FedEx (in addition to any shipping cost incurred internally by Amazon).

It will typically cost almost five dollars to ship a book. This can be quite large relative to the cost of the book itself. On the other hand, it can save an hour of time driving to the bookstore, finding the book, and getting through the checkout. If consumers can purchase several books at a time so that the shipping costs get to within 10 percent of the value of the book, then the shipping costs become close to the sales-tax savings, and using the Web becomes cost-efficient. Amazon and other online booksellers have clearly benefited from this tax savings, but they are likely to find that cost-conscious consumers are apt to start shifting back to bricks-and-mortar sellers when the tax advantage expires.

Examples of Markets Likely to Resist the Internet Assault

The products that are likely to be poor candidates for Internet sales are those with high bulk relative to value, perishable products, experience products, and products providing instant gratification. What are some examples of these products?

Which products fit the "experience" mode and are thus unlikely to be sold over the Net? One example is clothing for which the fit is very important, clothing that the user hasn't specifically ordered before, and clothing that changes with fashions. On the other hand, clothing that is purchased regularly and that does not change much, for example, shoes, or clothing that doesn't go out of fashion, perhaps the type of products found in L.L. Bean catalogs, might be better sold over the Internet.

Automobiles, for which the "drive" and looks are important, are not likely to be sold over the Net. Homes, which are unique and nonhomogeneous, are unlikely to be sold over the Internet. That isn't to say that buyers might not use the Internet to whittle their search down to a small number of items, which then will be inspected the old-fashioned way.

Perishability removes most prepared foods from the list of serious candidates for major Internet transformations of markets. McDonald's, for example, is not going to make Big Macs in some central location and FedEx them to your home. This would be nonsensical. The time for delivery would be far too high (in part because prepared foods are often in the "instant gratification" category). Additionally, the transportation costs would be too high, particularly if McDonald's were concerned about keeping their products from losing all of their taste and/or basic healthfulness.

Neither would most purveyors of frozen food be likely to shift completely to Web-based sales since no seller has a complete enough line of products to cover the tastes of consumers efficiently. Part of the reason for this is that there is a fixed cost to going shopping, even on the Web, and consumers wouldn't want to place numerous orders for each brand and type of frozen food. Supermarkets have arisen to allow consumers to take advantage of economies of scale in the shopping experience and in the delivery experience.[6]

A similar analysis can also be used to explain why most clothing, automobiles, furniture, pet food, and prescription drugs are not likely to migrate to the Web. Automobiles are an interesting special case, particularly since there is a web of state laws protecting current dealers from competition.

Grocery Items

Several factors are at work making grocery items very unlikely candidates for products that can be successfully sold on the Web. The items tend to be bulky relative to their value, making them poor candidates for economical delivery. Perishable and frozen items cannot be left on the porch, particularly in the summer, thus requiring pinpoint delivery times, which is necessarily a more expensive form of delivery. Various items such as fruit and meat are experience products in the sense that consumers like to look at or squeeze the items. Given these factors, which indicate that groceries are not likely to be a major online market, it is unfortunate that Web grocers were one of the more publicized and among the better funded set of Internet start-ups.

Early prognostications were rosy. In late 1999 the two leading online grocers, Webvan and HomeGrocer, had market capitalizations that appeared to be in excess of $5 billion, which compared favorably with the number-four bricks-and-mortar chain, Winn-Dixie, which had a $3 billion market capitalization (on sales of $14 billion). The values were even within striking distance of Albertson's $11 billion market capitalization (on $31 billion in sales) even though the online grocers generated sales of only about $100 million and generated no profit.[7] Here is a typical upbeat prognostication:

> Why the flurry over groceries? With sales of $450 billion—not including over-the-counter drugs and prepared meals, which add another $100 billion or so—it's too rich a marketplace to ignore. Zona Research estimates there are 31 online companies going after a share of the more than $7.5 billion online consumers are expected to spend on toothpaste, ketchup, and other grocery items by the year 2003. They include Amazon.com-backed HomeGrocer.com and first mover Peapod.
>
> According to Jupiter Communications' Ken Cassar, while grocery stores as they exist in the brick-and-mortar world are a low-margin business, the gross margins for groceries are high: 25 percent to 30 percent, compared with 20 percent for books and 17 percent to 18 percent for music. "The gross is good; it's the fixed expenses that drag down grocery sellers," Cassar said.
>
> And that leaves plenty of room for some bright, nimble Internet start-up to figure out a way to cash in on the inefficiencies that bog down brick-and-mortar competitors.[8]

Note the hubris in the last sentence, which nicely encapsulates the heady feelings of the times. Instead of delineating the advantages that the Internet might bring to consumers and producers who adopted it, the claim is that inherent "inefficiencies" would be reduced. Forget the fact that these grocery companies had been slugging it out for decades and that any inherent inefficiencies would likely have been reduced by this competition. Forget the fact that Wal-Mart, the king of retailer efficiency, was entering the supermarket business in a big way. Instead, a bunch of kids with MBAs were going to outsmart prior generations because they knew how to use the Internet better.

Note also the claims about profitability. The profitability comparison that the Jupiter analysts make is with "gross" margins on sales, which are reported to be much higher than net margins. But this, of course, is a result of the fact that a good part of the cost of a grocery store is the physical plant needed to warehouse the merchandise before it is sold. Gross margins must be higher; it couldn't be any other way. The claim that Jupiter analysts seem to be making is that Web grocers wouldn't need anywhere near the amount of physical plant that offline grocers would, certainly a questionable assumption since online grocers would need a fleet of delivery trucks not required by offline grocers and would still need freezers and space to warehouse their products, even if not quite to the same degree as offline grocers.

The more fundamental mistake of the Jupiter analysts, however, is one that has nothing to do with Web business versus offline business. This is the claim that either gross or net margins have any relevance whatsoever for investors in this business. Margins on sales do not tell you anything about the profitability of an industry. I discuss this in more detail in the section of chapter 5 entitled "Understanding Profit Margins."

Several business models were put forward in an attempt to make online grocery shopping a viable market. The major players were/are HomeGrocer, Peapod, and Webvan.[9]

Webvan and HomeGrocer intended to reinvent the grocery business as it was currently known. Webvan, for example, tried to change some of the underlying economics of warehousing and transportation costs by automating warehouses and developing special trucks. It is always possible that there could be an inefficiency in the present system. It does seem unlikely though. Any inefficiencies in the present system would have presented profit opportunities to anyone willing to experiment, and it is unclear what advantage Internet entrepreneurs would have in sniffing out such inefficiencies. For example, most people shop for pretty much the same food week after week. If home delivery was a potential goldmine, why wouldn't the idea have taken off using fax, telephone, or mail? Why was it thought that it required the Internet to make home delivery successful?

The answer, I believe, is that when people are throwing money at virtually any idea or company with an "e" in front of its name, it seems worthwhile going forward with any long shot. In Webvan's case it seems clear that its backers believed in the model, but its backers were not the seasoned businessmen they thought they were. In many cases they were young and rich from previous investments that had more to do with being in the right place at the right time than with any long-term business sense. They should have had the sense to not believe their press clippings. Warren Buffett, on the other hand, the famous investor and Berkshire Hathaway CEO, was a seasoned investor with the sense to stay out of investments that didn't make any sense to him.

Peapod, at least early on, attempted to use existing grocery stores and their distribution centers and to leverage off this distribution system to provide home delivery, using the Internet as an ordering mechanism for consumers. This is what I referred to as a partially transforming Internet makeover since the incumbent distribution system used to get the products to the retailer was left intact, and only the order-taking and final portion of delivery was altered. Because Peapod never was a complete Internet player, its stock (or in this case, its imputed value from the private sale of a portion of the stock) never entered the stratospheric heights that other Internet stocks such as Webvan were able to achieve.

To understand what the Web grocers were up against, it is necessary to have the proper level of respect for the current offline grocers. This is a business that has been competitive and has seen many venerable chains such as Grand Union, Pathmark, and A&P find their fortunes declining. This is a mature business where the identities of the leaders have been changing and where mergers have led to major shifts in market shares. It is a market that has proven tough to crack, even for the most fearsome foes, such as Wal-Mart and Costco. The market leaders have proved themselves to be fearsome competitors. And they certainly can, or should be, presumed efficient in their distribution systems given the current state of the art.

This means that it is reasonable to believe that the distribution methods that have evolved must be quite efficient, or else a smart competitor would have been able to make great inroads. It means that the pricing strategies, in-house labeling of products, advertising, and so forth were probably state-of-the-art. It means that the concept of having consumers shop and bring their products home in their cars was one that resonated well with the public.

Nevertheless, there is always room for innovation. The question was whether the innovation brought about by Web retailers was something desired and valued by consumers. The other question is why anyone would expect an innovation in distribution to be developed by a young Web entrepreneur as opposed to someone experienced in distribution.

The innovations promised by the Web grocers were (a) online ordering and purchase, (b) home delivery, and, in some instances, (c) efficiency in distribution. Prior to the Internet, home delivery was possible and even was popular in some localities such as Manhattan. One needs to ask why home delivery of groceries had not already become established, and what the Internet could do to alter the equation.

Home delivery requires ordering food, and although there are thousands of possible items, most families make repeat purchases from a much smaller set of products. Filling out a hard-copy form might be somewhat less convenient than ordering over the Internet, and updating the forms to reflect changing prices would also be more costly, but it is hard to imagine that this enhancement in ordering ease would be of such crucial importance as to be the key difference between success and failure.

In principle, offline grocers could have shoppers send in their orders and pick up their filled orders later in the day. This would shorten the time spent in the store by the average shopper although the drive and pickup would still remain. There doesn't seem to be much demand for this on the part of consumers, at least not as revealed by the behavior of grocers.

The crucial distinction between regular supermarket shopping and that offered by online grocers is (b) delivery of the product. This is where the true timesaving for consumers takes place. The Web grocers substitute the time of their paid employees (and the cost of this time) for the time of the consumer in shopping and delivery. The real question is in part whether most or many consumers prefer to make this substitution of an employee's time for their own time and also whether they find it more convenient to go shopping when they have the time as opposed to taking delivery of food items in a specific time period. Some consumers probably value the ability to make last-minute decisions as they go through the aisles of a supermarket, and others might actually enjoy shopping. For these consumers or under these circumstances, Internet shopping is clearly not going to be preferred.

There are compelling economic reasons why grocery delivery has always been a small niche market, and the Internet does nothing to change those reasons.

It is instructive to compare online grocers to pizza delivery stores. Delivery has become the predominant form of pizza purchase. Consumers are apparently willing to pay someone to deliver the pizza as opposed to picking it up themselves. Wouldn't these same consumers also favor delivery of grocery items? There are several important differences that push the answer to this question into the negative. Pizza is simple to order. Pizza delivery occurs almost immediately after ordering, so the recipient doesn't have to worry about being home when the delivery occurs. Pizza delivery is cheaper than grocery delivery since the pizza vendor doesn't have to purchase a fleet of vehicles. This last point is worthy of some additional analysis.

Economists often talk about capacity problems as "peak-load" problems. One example is electric companies trying to meet demand on very hot summer days when the peak demand can surpass the capacity of the generating stations. A similar problem occurs with food delivery. Most people are home at night and on weekends. They are likely to prefer to have groceries delivered at those times. At other times, the number of deliveries is likely to be much smaller. If a Web grocer buys a fleet of vehicles to meet the peak demand, then there will be a great deal of unused capacity sitting around during other parts of the day. This makes the cost of delivery much higher than if this wasted capacity didn't exist.

Pizza delivery handles the peak-load problem by hiring drivers who use their own cars. They hire drivers to match expected demand so there is no wasted cost in vehicles (or drivers) sitting around during non-peak times. Online grocers have not tried to emulate this strategy, presumably out of concern that their vehicles need to meet special standards to ensure that delivered products arrive in good condition. Presumably, consumers wouldn't be happy seeing someone drive up in his beat-up Civic and pull the groceries out of the beat-up trunk, scooping up fallen items in the process. Also, it would not be fun to get melted ice cream that had sat in the unrefrigerated Civic. This understandable concern for quality imposes considerably higher costs.

Instead, online grocers have spiffy new vans with refrigeration units to keep frozen food from thawing. This requires that the fleet of vans be quite expensive. If these vans sit around unused for the better part of the day, online grocers are faced with much higher costs than if they could alleviate the peak-load problem.

In principle, the peak-load problem can be eliminated if consumer demand can be massaged so that it becomes evenly spread out during the day. There are several ways in which this could be brought about. One method might be to charge higher delivery prices during peak periods to discourage consumers from requesting those times. The problem here is that consumers might switch to the alternative of old-fashioned shopping, eschewing the Internet altogether as a method of purchasing groceries.

Another method would be to use technology to allow the delivered food to be kept fresh and safe when it is delivered at a time that is not convenient for consumers. This has been tried in several instances. In California, Web-grocers have installed locked refrigeration units outside the homes of customers so that deliveries can be made throughout the day or night at a time convenient for the seller without serious degradation of the grocery items for the consumer, who then gets to shelve the product at a convenient time. This is obviously a very expensive solution. Consumers often change their minds about their vendors. It would obviously be uneconomical to go to the expense of installing these refrigeration units at the home of a consumer who will only purchase food for two weeks. Also, different consumers have different percentages of frozen food, meaning that the outdoor units might sometimes not adequately hold all the food items unless there were a great deal of excess capacity in these units, further increasing their cost. This solution obviously raises the cost differential between delivered grocery items and picked-up grocery items, making the old-fashioned shopping experience relatively more attractive.

Finally, Webvan claimed that it was going to revolutionize the grocery distribution system.

> Executives at Webvan say the company will have a competitive advantage because of giant warehouses, which will make it much faster and easier to process a large volume of orders. "We've got a significantly more efficient business model," said Chris Manella, Webvan's vice president of marketing. The planned giant warehouses will also let the company store a larger selection of products than its competitors, Manella said.[10]

This was a claim of monumental hubris. It is thus not surprising that online Web grocers have fallen by the wayside. Home-Grocer was bought by Webvan, which itself went out of business as the most well-financed e-commerce bankruptcy to date.[11]

Automobiles

The future of Web-based automobile sales is clouded by myriad state and local regulations controlling who can sell automobiles, where they can be located, and various other aspects of the business (see the section entitled "Implications for Internet Companies" in chapter 5 for more information).

In addition to the problems posed by these regulations, there are numerous other difficulties in trying to sell automobiles on the Web. The key problem is that automobiles are quite clearly and strongly "experience goods." Few people would buy an automobile without being able to sit in it to have a test-drive of at least a similar model if not the actual specific vehicle. There is no way to recreate this experience on the Web. Therefore, assuming that automobile producers can overcome the various regulations regarding automobile sales, we can expect that Internet sales would require local showrooms for automobile inspection and driving even if the ordering is done over the Internet.

If this is to be the case, it is unclear that automobile companies would wish to forgo the high-pressure sales tactics they have found so successful in the past. If automobile companies were to keep salesmen, the consumer wouldn't be able to actually order the automobile over the Internet, and the "showrooms" would be virtually, or perhaps I should say "actually," identical to current showrooms.

The concept of Internet sales implies take-it-or-leave-it pricing, where prices are posted and no negotiations are possible. This is how Saturn automobiles are sold, but this is quite unusual in the industry and would require a significant change. Once again, as I have repeated throughout the book, it is important not to underestimate the value of those institutions that have survived and evolved over many years since there are usually good economic reasons for such survival. It is reasonable to presume that employing salespeople and high-pressure tactics increases the profits of automobile dealers; otherwise, this technique would have died out long ago.

Furniture

Furniture would seem to be a product extremely poorly suited to Internet sales. It is heavy and bulky, although not inexpensive. It is an experience good—who would purchase a sofa without the opportunity to sit on it?

One might imagine that furniture delivery would share some characteristics with automobile delivery—showrooms for the furniture but ordering on the Internet and delivery either at the showroom or through a shipper, depending on which was more economical.

There are many small furniture manufacturers, and a Web site would have to deal with a large number of them in the hopes of having a large variety of products. Of course, aggregation is one of the advantages of Web retailing. It would, however, be impractical to have numerous showrooms with display items for hundreds of different manufacturers in each locality so that consumers could experience the product; it would then be unclear what the savings might be relative to traditional furniture retailers.

Further, it is difficult to imagine that shipping from the factory would be more economical than shipping from a showroom. If it were, that is how we might have expected the industry to have evolved in the first place. Of course, if the companies selling furniture over the Internet tried to sell a very wide variety, that would limit their ability to use showrooms. Once again, we need to be respectful of the institutions that have emerged and flourished in a competitive environment as furniture showrooms did.

Furniture sales were tried but foundered early on.[12] In an MSNBC article in March of 2000, Jane Weaver suggests that consumer complaints might be the undoing of online furniture deliverers such as Furniture.com; she catalogs the woes of a handful of customers with horror stories of furniture that was undelivered for months. Nevertheless, she ended her story with this projection from Forrester Research: "Online furniture sales should top $3.9 billion in 2004, up from $268 million in 1999." On November 20, 2000, Furniture.com filed for bankruptcy.[13]

Prescription Drugs

Prescription drugs can be dichotomized into distinct groups: those that are purchased on an ongoing basis to mitigate a chronic disorder and those that are purchased unpredictably when someone suddenly becomes ill. Drugs in the former group are better candidates for Internet selling than those in the latter group. Drugs used to help alleviate or cure unpredictable illnesses are like impulse goods—the consumer wants immediate consumption (relief). After all, who wants to remain sick any longer than necessary? With overnight delivery being so expensive and still significantly slower than the current system of using one's corner drugstore, it seems extremely unlikely that consumers would turn to Internet drugstores to fill prescriptions for unpredictable illnesses.

Even for drugs that are ordered with regularity, however, it is difficult to see any strong advantage held by the Internet store, particularly relative to a telephone-based system. The consumer does not have to choose between a large selection of products since it is the doctor who determines which drugs the patient is going to purchase, thus ruling out the advantage of the Internet's ability to provide information better than does a phone call. The prescription still needs to be filled and shipped by a licensed pharmacist housed in some building somewhere, so there is little saving there for an Internet company. The doctor's prescription needs to be sent to the pharmacist, Internet or not. The Internet company's ability to take orders twenty-four hours a day might be an advantage, but not a very large one. Therefore, for prescription drugs, at least, it is unclear that Internet pharmacies have much of a reason to exist except as a minor convenience to customers who may prefer them to the phone, perhaps to avoid busy calls during peak times.

The Nature of Selling on the Net

The success of companies sponsoring auctions or other unusual forms of pricing, such as eBay, Yahoo, and Priceline, have caused some commentators to suggest that auctions are going to be playing an increasing role in future sales. For example, Clay Shirky, a professor of media studies at Hunter College recently opined in the pages of the *Wall Street Journal* that "the real importance of the name-your-price model . . . [is that it is] a harbinger of a revolution being wrought by the information economy: the disappearance of fixed retail prices."[14]

This seems very unlikely to me. Again, too little respect is paid to the more "traditional" pricing methods. These methods did not arise by happenstance. Instead, they evolved and changed as the economy and society changed. The Internet, I believe, is going to have the exact opposite effect—likely reducing rather than increasing the current variability in prices.

The Evolution of the Current Pricing System

Did you ever wonder why third-world countries have bazaars and shops where bargaining is considered the norm, and yet this is so very rare in most Western shopping centers? Or why the prices are simply posted on the aisle at your local mall and grocery store instead of being negotiated?

It isn't a cultural difference.

Historically, bargaining was common in what is now the Western or developed world until the very modern period. The developed countries were much more rural than they are now. There were no shopping centers or department stores. The shopkeepers often knew who their clients were. Some degree of bargaining was common.

Since the seller spent more time bargaining than did most of the buyers, bargaining generally worked to the seller's advantage. Since the store owner was also the primary bargainer, there was no difficulty in providing sufficient incentives for the bargainer who was representing the store to try to maximize revenues and prices—the bargainer and the store owner were one and the same.

The confluence of several factors helped to bring about the demise of bargaining. As stores became larger, the owner couldn't do all the selling, and it was costly to provide the right incentives for the sales help to bargain with customers. First, the sales help would have to be on some sort of commission or its equivalent to provide them sufficient incentive to bargain with full energy. Second, the sales help would have to be reasonably bright to be able to engage in such bargaining. These two factors implied that sales help would have to be relatively well paid given the characteristics that were required. Further, the invention of the cash register made it more economical for less skilled help to work in a store (math skills were no longer a requirement).[15]

Increases in income and specialization in production have led to many more items being purchased today than was the case in previous centuries. We are individually much less self-sufficient. At one time it was common for families, the majority of whom lived an agrarian existence, to produce much of their own food and simple goods. As incomes and progress raced ahead, specialization in production became more and more common, requiring more and more reliance on market transactions to purchase items that had previously been made at home.[16]

We also have much more disposable income with which to purchase the products that are available in our markets. Higher disposable income not only increases the number of items we tend to purchase but also makes leisure time more valuable since it is during our leisure time that we get to consume the products we have purchased. The high cost of time has made haggling over the price of ordinary items very inconvenient for most individuals.

At the same time that incomes were rising and stores were getting larger, transportation costs were falling, thanks to the invention and mass adoption of automobiles and the like, allowing consumers to comparison shop more easily. The high cost of time and the low cost of information made it uneconomical for sellers in modern economies to engage in price negotiations except for the most expensive items such as automobiles.

Imagine, if you will, haggling with the checkout clerk over the prices of the items in your supermarket basket. Checkout clerks, for one, would need far more sophistication than they typically have and would also need a different form of payment, or they wouldn't have the proper incentive to try to get the highest price.

Bored high-school kids earning six to eight dollars per hour are not the ideal individuals to engage in hardy negotiations representing the store. Also, imagine how time-consuming such negotiations would be. It would make getting stuck in line behind someone with lots of manufacturers' coupons (and paying by check) seem like a cakewalk. Customers, particularly in such colorful locales as Brooklyn, would likely riot.

Now duplicate this experience in drugstores, restaurants, department stores, and gas stations, and you can quickly see that haggling over price would just be insane. Modern Western countries have moved in the exact opposite direction. We have drive-throughs for almost everything. Don't bother getting out of your car. Get your coffee, your lunch, your photographs, and your dry-cleaning, all without leaving your car. The raison d'être for all these drive-throughs is not to avoid breathing the outside air but to save time. Saving time is one of the great motifs of our modern Western world.

Posting fixed prices, in its own way, achieves the same end. No negotiations. No concern that you might not get the product as long as it is in stock. From a timesaving point of view, posted prices are extremely functional. The Internet is not going to send us back to the bazaar—that would be a step backward.

Posted prices are not ideal, however, for the seller who is narrowly interested in maximizing revenues. Exactly why is explained in the next section.

The Concept of Price Discrimination

Haggling allows sellers to size up the buyer. Since sellers normally spend more time selling than buyers do buying, sellers will tend to have more experience when haggling. Sellers with poor haggling abilities in a haggling world will not long remain sellers. The most common example of haggling still found in modern society is the automobile dealer.

Automobile salesmen get paid as a function of how high a price they can get consumers to pay. Making the sale is not the goal if it is achieved at a low price. Making a sale at a high price is the goal. Automobile salesmen use various tactics to convince consumers that there is only one car that is perfect for them, that it will be purchased by another consumer within a few minutes, and that they have been inadvertently offered too low a price—in fact, it is so low that the salesman might lose his job when the boss finds out. A charade is then often played out with the salesman feigning concern that his boss might not approve of the low price while the boss thinks it over. These staged meetings and confrontations between the salesmen and their supervisors, along with the high-pressure tactics used by the salesmen, are quite effective at closing deals, which is why they continue to be used. The process is so time-consuming and annoying that many consumers try to avoid these situations as they would try to avoid the plague.

But this activity serves the interests of the automobile dealer and perhaps even the interests of society. That is because the dealer is engaging in what economists call "price discrimination." This just means that they are charging different prices to different customers, and if they are getting it right, they are charging higher prices to the customers who are willing to pay more. The maximum price consumers are willing to pay is known as a *reservation price*.[17] This is a well-worn subject that can be found in virtually any microeconomics text.

Price discrimination allows the seller to earn greater profits than would be possible if the same single price were charged to all customers. Even though the price discriminator makes more money, not all customers are harmed. Those customers who are unwilling to pay a high price would often be priced out of the market if only a single price were offered to all consumers. After all, even if the price that this low-reservation-price consumer will pay is greater than the production cost, potentially leading to a profitable sale, the seller will not charge this price to all users if there are many customers willing to pay a higher price. In this case, lowering the price so the low-reservation-price customer will buy the item decreases profits from the high-reservation-price customers by more than the gain from the new sales to the low-reservation-price customers. The single price that balances these forces and maximizes profits is known simply as the profit-maximizing price. This is a fundamental concept in introductory economics although students often get confused by the mathematics.[18]

When different prices can be charged, however, the seller doesn't lose money from the high-reservation-price customers when he attempts to bring low-reservation-price customers into the market since he can charge lower prices to only the individuals that he chooses.[19] That is why price discrimination can increase his profits. It also allows low-price customers into the market, and the net result may well be beneficial to society at large if it leads to greater total output being sold.[20]

Price discrimination is illegal under certain circumstances, but only if the customers are businesses that compete with one another. Under the law, sellers of final goods to regular consumers can price-discriminate to their heart's content. What's the difference between these two instances of price discrimination? No economic difference at all. It is entirely a political decision.

The point of this foray into what is likely to be for many readers a painful memory from their college economics course, is that haggling allows price discrimination and, everything else being equal, should prove profitable for the seller.

But haggling is also expensive for the seller, who needs a staff of trained and motivated vipers if the haggling is to prove successful in raising revenues. For almost all products in the United States, the extra costs are greater than the additional revenues that would be generated, so haggling has largely disappeared. It exists in the case of automobiles because the items are very expensive and because each automobile tends to have a somewhat unique set of options, making it difficult for the high-price customers to realize that they overpaid, an important precondition of price discrimination if it is to be truly successful.[21]

Posted prices, although price discrimination is forsaken, are a very cheap way of selling products.[22] It is no surprise that retailing with posted prices is now the dominant form of selling—it makes economic sense.

So what is the meaning of online auctions? Are they a form of price discrimination? Do they benefit sellers or buyers? Why do auctions exist on the Internet but not in bricks-and-mortar markets?

What About Auctions?

Sellers should only wish to engage in auctions if they can receive a higher price than would be available through the alternative, some form of posted price. But buyers, being aware of posted prices elsewhere, should not be willing to pay higher prices in auctions. This is a conundrum that should keep auctions from becoming a dominant form of retailing on the Internet.

There is one fly in the ointment, but it isn't likely to play that large a role. Consumers currently seem to value the entertainment aspect of auctions, and the thrill of the auction might make them willing to buy at auctions even if it means paying a slightly higher price.

Interestingly, in the current excitement brought about by auctions, some buyers have been paying more than they would have paid purchasing the identical items sold at retail. However, as this information becomes more readily known (through outlets such as *Consumer Reports*), consumers will become more wary of auctions, and auctions are likely to be relegated to those items for which auctions make the most sense—items that are not currently being sold at retail.

Auctions are a good way to sell out-of-season, clearance, and one-of-a-kind merchandise, and for these reasons may largely replace bricks-and-mortar discounters who have tended to specialize in such merchandise. Net auctions are also likely to displace the classified-advertising market, since these are usually heterogeneous products. The Internet allows easy searching, and the Internet allows national or international users to enter the market.

Markets that were too thin at local geographic levels (meaning that too few buyers or sellers existed to ensure that the price went to a reasonable level) can function more efficiently on the Internet.

Auctions, however, are not a good way for ordinary new products to be sold. The increased availability of price information made possible by the Internet should make it increasingly difficult to sell new, homogeneous products at differential prices. It will just be too easy for consumers to compare prices and to know what is the best available price for a product.[23]

Notes

1. I really am not trying to pick on Mary Meeker. But her very lofty position during the Internet mania would appear to justify this attention to her. This quote can be found on page 123 of their presentation "An Internet Overview" found in the May 2000 issue of *The Technology Primer*, Morgan Stanley Dean Witter, which can be found at: *http://www.morganstanley.com/institutional/eInterpriseSoftware/techprimer/primer2.pdf*.

2. E. S. Browning, "Is There a Rationale That Can Justify New Economy's Lofty Stock Prices?", *Wall Street Journal*, March 23, 2000.

3. Q&A with Jeff Bezos, *BusinessWeek Online*, May 21, 1999. I should note that Bezos, in this interview, claims that increasing returns is not central to his business but that quality of service to consumers is. His view on this issue seems quite sophisticated. My major disagreement with his analysis is that he believes that the old distribution system is outdated for many retail businesses and can be improved upon by Internet companies.

4. This argument was first proposed by Lester Telser. See "Why do Manufacturers Want Fair-Trade Laws?" *Journal of Law and Economics* 3 (1960): 86.

5. Troy Wolverton "Economic, political shifts revive calls for e-tail levies" CNET News.com, October 30, 2001 available at *http://news.cnet.com/news/0-1007-201-7705080-0.html*.

6. The economy in the delivery experience includes economies of shipment from the manufacturer to the retailer and economies in the delivery of the product from the retailer to the consumers.

7. George Anders, "HomeGrocer Raises $100 Million In Additional Venture Funding," *Wall Street Journal* (online version), November 2, 1999.

8. Connie Guglielmo and Edward Cone, "Will Online Groceries Deliver Profits?" *Inter@ctive Week*, September 24, 1999.

9. I leave off the dot-com ".com" extender on each of these companies to simplify the names.

10. Joanna Glasner, "Webvan's $1 Billion Soup Job," *Wired News*, July 9, 1999, available at *http://www.wired.com/news/business/0,1367, 20646,00.html.*

11. "Online Grocer Webvan Shuts Down" MSNBC, July 9, 2001 available at *http://www.msnbc.com/local/knbc/nbcx0tl0yoc.asp.*

12. Jane Weaver, "Can Furniture.com Deliver? Customer Complaints Cloud IPO Outlook," MSNBC, March 1, 2000. *http://wwwpub. utdallas.edu/liebowit/weaver.pdf.*

13. Go to the Web site *www.furniture.com.*

14. "Haggling Goes High-Tech," *Wall Street Journal,* April 10, 2000.

15. It has been claimed that the cash register is what has led to pricing just below even numbers (i.e., items with ninety-nine cents as the last two digits). This ensured that the cash register had to be used, making it difficult for employees to pocket the sales revenue without leaving a trail.

16. Although the text might seem to imply that increases in income led to specialization, the causation largely goes the other way. As individuals specialized in particular productive activities, this allowed incomes to rise.

17. Of course, no one wants to pay a higher price, but we each have a maximum price we are willing to pay. Those with high reservation prices are the ones who pay higher prices if the seller engages in successful price discrimination.

18. The rule is simply to equate marginal revenue with marginal cost, but many students have difficulty with marginal concepts, which are often expressed in terms of derivatives.

19. Price discrimination is usually described in terms of charging different prices to groups of customers where the groups have different degrees of responsiveness (elasticities) to price changes. My description in the text is somewhat closer to what is known as perfect price discrimination, which occurs when each customer is charged a price just equal to that customer's maximum willingness to pay. The impacts of haggling are better described with this analogy.

20. Actually, economists are interested in efficiency, measured in this simple case by the quantity of output sold. Price discrimination usually increases efficiency, so defined, even if consumers are made worse off. Economics doesn't choose between consumers and producers. Therefore a transfer of wealth from one group to the other is not considered relevant from an efficiency point of view.

21. In the economics literature, price discrimination can only succeed when "arbitrage" is impossible, meaning that middlemen cannot arise to purchase the low-priced items and resell them to the high-price individuals. Keeping consumers in the dark about prices makes arbitrage less likely.

22. Even with posted prices, motivated consumers can negotiate a deal on items that are fairly expensive, such as furniture or appliances.

23. Although largely ignored here, for readings on B2B models, see D. Lucking-Reiley and D. Spulber, "Business to Business Electronic Commerce," *Journal of Economic Perspectives*, Winter 2001, 55–69.

Chapter 5

The Value-Profit Paradox

The Cruelty of Competition and Internet Margins

This chapter makes three points. The first is that great profits do not necessarily flow from creating great value. The second is that competition is very, very bad for profits. Since the Internet is expected to have fewer entry barriers than one finds in many bricks-and-mortar markets, this bodes poorly for high profits. The third is that, since Internet retailers provide very low value-added, margins will be very small.

The Internet is going to create great value. That is not in dispute. Who gets that value, however, is not so easy to predict.

Value is typically shared between consumers and producers. First, consumers derive net value when they get to purchase products for which they pay less than they would actually be willing to pay. Even though I pay two dollars for a Big Mac, I would be willing to pay more—perhaps three dollars—if faced with the stark choice of handing over three dollars or not getting my Big Mac. The total sum of these differentials between the maximum that consumers are willing to pay and what they actually pay is known as the "surplus" that consumers receive.[1] Second, producers usually receive prices that are higher than the minimum that they would be willing to accept, another form of surplus.[2]

It is possible that the surplus created by the Internet will go disproportionately to either consumers or producers. If producers invest too little (from the perspective of economic efficiency), more of the surplus will go to them. Their small investment makes it more difficult for consumers to get all of the Internet content and shopping they want, allowing producers to keep prices high.[3] Monopoly is a particular form of investing too little. Producers usually attempt to figure out ways to restrict the amount of investment that occurs, and they often rely on the government to restrict this investment, as discussed below.

If producers invest too much, more of the surplus will go to consumers. Competition is what forces producers not to invest too little. Overinvestment occurs when producers misjudge the market and provide too much of what they are selling, forcing prices down. Overinvestment is not likely to be more than a temporary phenomenon since it tends to drive companies out of business. Extreme overinvestment can cause the surplus earned by producers to turn negative, which is why it tends to lead to the exit of companies from the industry.

Investments that companies make in industries are not really all that different than prospecting for gold in a gold rush. These prospecting odds are much greater when few people know about the gold than if everyone knows about it. This simple point seemed to be almost entirely overlooked in the recent overheated Internet market, but it had strongly negative implications for profits. At its height, practically everyone was headed for the fabled gold, but they were looking for it in the ether instead of in yonder hills.

Just about everyone recognized that the Internet would create value. Just how much value would be created was the sixty-four-thousand-dollar question. Many thought the value was going to be enormous, unlike anything that came before it. This is why the media focused so much energy and attention on a story that would normally have been expected to remain hidden in the business section rather than appearing on the front page. This is why *Time* magazine named as its 1999 man of the year an entrepreneur whose company had not come close to making a penny of profit.[4] There was surely a large amount of hype in all of this.

In addition, as we saw in chapter 3, many academics, business analysts, and investment strategists believed that being first was a key component to success. That is why companies stampeded to get a piece of the action. This is why venture capitalists were lining up at the doors of every start-up dot-com, hoping to get a piece of the action.

In the economics literature there is a phenomenon known as a patent race, in which companies may overinvest in an attempt to get the patent, which goes only to the first company, leaving the laggards with nothing to show for their efforts. The combination of an overhyped Internet phenomenon and the race to be first led to an overinvestment in virtually anything having to do with the Internet.

The end result, at least in the short run, is that the value created by the Internet is not being split very evenly. In fact, it seems relatively fair to say that overinvestment has removed any surplus from producers.[5] That is why the Internet landscape is strewn with so many dead carcasses, with many other companies in intensive care.[6]

Consumers have benefited as they voluntarily adopted this new technology. After all, people wouldn't make the switch unless they were better off.[7] They also benefited from producer largesse during the wild period when producers were intentionally subsidizing consumers by selling products below cost, a situation that could not have remained in equilibrium although it didn't seem so unlikely to many at that time.

Notice that I am not saying that some producers will not do very well, only that the typical or average producer will not necessarily do well even though the market is growing. This is what happened to DRAM (memory chip) manufacturers who ran into very low profits even in the face of ever-increasing sales of computers and an ever-increasing appetite for memory. The DRAM companies frequently overinvested in chip fabrication plants.

It is also important to understand that the profit generation in product markets works just the opposite of stock market profits. In the case of stocks, the more people who jump on the bandwagon, the higher the stock price goes and the greater everyone's profits. For companies who are competing with one another, however, the more that enter the industry, the lower everyone's profits turn out to be. The willingness of the capital market to fund so many untested Internet companies and the enormous publicity and expectations surrounding the Internet augured poorly for the likelihood that these companies would do well in the real market.

The Diamond-Water Paradox

The dichotomy between value creation and dollar generation can be traced to a famous analysis known as the diamond-water paradox. The meaning of economic value, and how markets translate (or fail to translate) such value into revenue, profit, and wealth, is at the heart of this issue.

Think for a moment about water (air would be an equally good example). How valuable is water? We need only notice that all known forms of life would die without water to reach the obvious conclusion that water must be very valuable. But does this large value translate into revenues and wealth? Have any entrepreneurs made great wealth from the sale of water? Are any great companies, like AT&T, IBM, or Microsoft, based upon the sale of water? The negative answers to these questions is consistent with the common observation that water is normally treated as a "throw-away" type of item. No one gets upset if someone wastes a few gallons of water, unless they happen to be in a desert or have had a temporary drought. The reason that water is treated so cavalierly is that water has a low price.

That a product can be so valuable and yet at the same time

so cheap is the essence of the paradox. We need not spend time examining the flip side that completes the paradox—i.e., the fact that diamonds do not have much value but are very expensive.

The paradox is solved, or explained, by understanding that the generation of total value has little to do with market revenues or prices. The laws of supply and demand, when taken together, imply that price is determined by the value of the *last* unit consumed, the last unit being known in economic parlance as the marginal unit.

In the case of water, the first gallon of water per day per person is extremely valuable since people use several gallons for drinking, washing, watering plants, etc. But if every person were to have a stockpile of ten thousand gallons a week, the value of an additional gallon of water, the ten thousand and first gallon, would be very low. Ten thousand gallons a week would take care of just about every conceivable use that a person might have within a week, so an additional gallon would be worth about zero.

Market prices are formed by the interaction of supply and demand. Although the demand for water is enormous, reflecting water's tremendous value, the supply is larger yet, causing the value of the last consumed unit of water to be very low. Thus water has a very low price. This also explains other instances in which prices don't seem to reflect overall value, such as the fact that truck drivers might get paid more than schoolteachers or that finance professors get paid more than (other) economists. Teaching may, from society's vantage point, be a more valuable activity than driving trucks, but if there is a larger supply of teachers so that an additional teacher brings less additional value than that brought by another truck driver, then truck drivers will have higher wages. Not only do markets work this way, but it can be demonstrated that it would be less efficient if prices were related to something other than the marginal value, such as, for example, the average value of a product.[8]

The point of this example is to illustrate how it can be that a product might provide enormous value but very little in the way of revenue or profit.[9] The very abundance of air and water makes it impossible to generate wealth in spite of the great value created. Therefore, the creation of great value is not by itself the key to producing profits.

This is of importance when trying to understand the financial implications of the Internet. Just because it produces great value does not mean that it will also produce great wealth.

The Cruelty of Competition and Attempts to Subvert It

The second key factor relating to the revenues and profits likely to flow from activities conducted on the Internet concerns the level of competition. The more competitive an environment, the more difficult it is to generate profits. I cannot overstate the importance of this.

What do I mean by competition? The key elements are whether other companies can enter the industry easily if they desire to compete with incumbent companies and whether it is easy or difficult to mimic what the incumbent companies have already accomplished.

This differs slightly from the typical economics textbook definition of competition. In most economics texts, a model of perfect competition includes free entry and exit, free information about prices and production processes, and a large number of very small companies. The main difference in these definitions is that the definition I am using doesn't require a very large number of very small companies.[10] Economists generally understand that markets can be very competitive even without a very large number of very small companies, and the latter assumption is usually included merely to make our models more tractable.

What does this mean for companies doing business on the Internet? Mainly that they are captives to the same forces that are at work in the bricks-and-mortar economy, and that competition is probably the single most important element controlling profitability in either venue.

Competition works to reduce prices and profits in an industry. Potential entrants examine the financial returns they might generate if they were to enter a particular industry. If they find a market where companies seem to be making easy money, they try to enter with all alacrity so that they too can take advantage of the high profits that are currently being earned. It is not the intention of the entrants to reduce the profits of those in the industry. Quite the opposite is true—they wish for profits to remain high. But as more companies enter a market in the hopes of striking it rich (earning above-normal returns on investment) the market becomes less profitable for all involved.

The market becomes less profitable because the entry of new companies and new productive capacity increases the output available for consumers to purchase. Where shortages may once have been common, now surpluses begin to replace them. We all know that a common response to surpluses is to start to hold "sales" events and begin marking down prices.

We can see this market behavior at work in the automobile market. In the 1980s American automobile manufacturers discovered that consumers' tastes were switching away from conventional automobiles and toward vans and minivans. Automobile manufacturers with enough foresight (or luck) to anticipate this trend found it easy to sell all the vehicles that they made. The Japanese automobile companies were late in catching this trend, and the leading producers of minivans, such as Chrysler, enjoyed high sales and profitability. The movement toward minivans was itself in part a function of the decreased cost of gasoline, which made ownership of these larger vehicles more affordable, and in part the result of baby boomers' moving into midlife and needing a large seating and towing capacity so that their children would no longer be cramped in the small sedans that had previously been popular.

Eventually, Japanese producers caught on to this trend and

produced their own line of minivans, decreasing the profitability of the minivan market as a whole. But by then the market had morphed once more, this time into one where sport-utility vehicles (SUVs) were now the hot items. These vehicles provided the space of a minivan without the stodgy association that was then being made between minivans and suburban moms carting around multiple children. With their high seats, large capacity, and more macho image, they attracted consumers who switched to them in droves. Again, the American automobile producers were there first, and they racked up impressive sales and profit figures. But competition reasserted itself when European and Japanese producers finally were able to produce their own models several years later. The market became flooded with models from Lexus, Mercedes, Suzuki, Isuzu, and Toyota, as well as new American entries from Lincoln, Cadillac, and others. Once again, competition reared its ugly head and worked to reduce profitability in the industry. Now, with gasoline prices highly variable and SUV capacity at an all-time high, we are likely to see profits in the SUV market come crashing down.

This decline in fortunes will not necessarily be true for all producers, however. Some producers always do a better job than others, and those who can better meet the demands of the market will earn higher returns than others. But the typical company, what is called the "representative" firm in economic models of competition, will no longer be able to earn above-normal profits in this market. And it will be competition that has removed those profits. This is why competition is so good for consumers but so bad for producers. The importance of competition can be seen by noting the resources that companies are willing to spend attempting to reduce the amount of competition they face.

American automobile producers have successfully lobbied for decades to restrict the imports of foreign automobiles. Farmers have for decades successfully lobbied to make it more difficult for competitors to enter and sell agricultural products; taxicab owners have succeeded in making it impossible for entry to occur in the taxicab business; doctors have imposed barriers restricting the number of new doctors that could be trained. In each of these markets, strenuous attempts have been and continue to be made to reduce competition by restricting entry. The purpose is to raise the prices and revenues of the sellers in those markets by weakening competitive pressures.

The taxi illustration is fascinating and is also a useful illustration of the impact of entry on competition and profits.

At one time, there was free entry into the market for individuals with vehicles willing to transport others for a fee. One by one, the governments in virtually every major city in the United States and Canada began to enact legislation making it illegal to engage in a taxicab type of service without having official permission from the government. The key element in the regulation is that this official permission is not dependent on having a safe cab or a good driving record. You can have modern and comfortable cabs, staffed by trained English-speaking drivers, knowledgeable about the geography of the city and with impeccable driving records, but that will be insufficient to allow you to enter the cab business. Instead you also need to have a piece of paper, known as a "medallion," which gives you governmental permission to be in the cab business.

"Surely," you ask, "anyone with clean cars and efficient drivers would receive a medallion, wouldn't they?" The answer is no. Medallions are not just given out, no matter how worthy a company might be. Instead, someone wishing to enter the taxi industry has to buy a medallion from someone else who is willing to leave the industry. In large cities, a medallion for a single cab costs several hundred thousand dollars, dwarfing the other costs of setting up a cab company.

What is the point of having medallions? It is not to ensure that cabs are safe and drivers knowledgeable since these requirements could be put in place without the need to resort to medallion ownership, and obviously these are not characteristics of the current taxicabs in major cities. Neither is it to guarantee that cab owners have sufficient financial resources to meet any suits that might arise in the courts should an accident occur. No, the medallion exists for one and only one purpose—to restrict competition in the taxicab business.

The beneficiaries of this system are actually the people who owned the cabs when the medallions were first instituted and when competition was first restricted because they were given the medallions for free. This phenomenon of giving away "rights" to compete in a market that is about to be made less competitive happens often enough that it has developed its own terminology. The process of allowing current market practitioners to receive a free "medallion," or right to be in the market, is known as "grand-fathering." The act of lobbying the government to grant rights such as these is known as "rent-seeking," where "rent" has the somewhat archaic meaning of "profit" that is still used by economists.

Government, you see, is the ultimate creator of monopoly. The best way to reduce competition is to make it illegal, something that governments have done for a very long time. They usually find some language to make it seem that they are helping consumers, when in fact they are doing the opposite. This is slightly different from copyrights and patents, policies that provide a form of monopoly enshrined in the Constitution for the purpose of providing inducements for the creation of more inventive and artistic activity.[11]

Sometimes, as was the case with the Hudson's Bay Company, a monopoly is granted in order to provide sufficient incentives for a company to explore new and potentially hostile territory. The claims-staking process in a gold rush serves a similar purpose. Much monopoly granting, however, serves a far narrower purpose—enriching some set of producers for no apparent reason other than enriching those producers. Taxicab medallions are an example of the latter form of enrichment.[12]

After the local city government creates a system of taxicab

medallions, it usually provides for a rather meager increase in the number of medallions—if any increase at all is granted. It almost goes without saying that the growth in the number of medallions is usually far smaller than the growth in demand for taxicab rides. This, therefore, makes the activity of providing taxicab rides more profitable than it would have been without the medallions.

The fact that, in New York City, it costs $300,000 for a piece of paper that gives permission to own a taxicab reveals the success of that program in generating profits.[13] After all, why would an investor pay anything beyond the cost of the cab, the insurance, the gasoline, and the driver? He must believe that, after covering all the costs associated with running a taxicab business, the cab must provide a profit, over time, of at least $300,000. Otherwise it would make no sense to pay that much for the medallion.

The irony in this is that competition once again reasserts it-self—not in the taxicab business, where the number of cabs is kept artificially low, but in the market for medallions, where competition is perfectly functional and works to increase the price of medallions to the point that the typical, or the "representative" cab owner, cannot expect to earn above-normal profits. The price of medallions, therefore, sops up all the profit because of the restricted competition in the taxicab business, and those who buy the medallions fail to earn any monopoly profit. All the profit goes to those who first received the medallions for free.

Don't think that taxicab medallions are some exotic throw-back to a previous era or some endangered species of poor government. When the government allocated television and radio frequencies, the same behavior took place. When the government restricts the acreage that farmers can plant, or guarantees minimum prices, this is the same type of policy. When the government restricts imports from abroad, this is part and parcel of the same policy.[14] The list could go on for many pages.

Implications for Internet Companies

So what does this have to do with the Internet, which is, after all, the putative topic of this book? There are two implications: first, that competition will erode the profits for many companies doing business on the Net and, second, that we should expect early entrants on the Net to cajole the government into trying to find some way to restrict competition on the Net just as it has restricted competition in so many other realms of enterprise.

One might imagine a form of licensing of Internet companies. Perhaps a form of government approval for the financial component of online purchases. Perhaps restrictions on new Web sites. If this sounds far-fetched—and I have to admit that it seems very odd to me—one needs to remember that automobile dealerships cannot just open up where they wish, and banks cannot just decide to locate where they want. Street merchants cannot sell when and where they want. For many years, many businesses could not open when they wanted and had to be closed on Sundays.

The selling of automobiles over the Internet is a good example. Many states have automobile franchise laws that restrict newcomers from entering the business of selling cars within certain local markets or from opening up within close proximity to an existing dealer (many states have similar regulations regarding banks). In many states, those laws have the effect of prohibiting anyone except a licensed dealer from selling cars over the Internet. That is why, when you try to buy a car online, you are most likely to have to go through a local dealer. If consumers wanted to purchase automobiles over the Internet (which, I argue in chapter 4, is unlikely), these laws would impede the market.[15]

Will the Internet prove to be an arena where government cannot regulate entry in such a way as to reduce competition? Certainly, optimistic libertarians have tended to view the Internet as an untamable environment, outside of the control of governments or of any large organizations. I suspect that they are going to be sorely disillusioned. The Internet can be regulated. And, unfortunately, it probably will be regulated in ways that go against the public's welfare.

Governments, whether local, national, or international, have shown their ability to work with companies to prevent competition. Perhaps the restriction on competition will come in the guise of protecting consumers from unscrupulous vendors. Perhaps it will come in the guise of minimum quality standards. Perhaps it will come by letting producer groups determine who is qualified to sell, as is the case for most professional licensing organizations. Perhaps it will be as simple as allowing the setting of standards that make it difficult for consumers to do simple comparison pricing while shopping on the Net.

But stay on the lookout. The Internet is ripe for competition-reducing activities. They have always arisen in other commercial activities. There is no reason to think that the Internet will be different.

Future Competition and Performance

The Internet entered the public's consciousness in the mid-1990s. In order for profits to flow in abundance, investment in Internet activities, which creates the supply of Internet products, needs to not overwhelm the very large value that will be created by the Internet.

The results for the first generation of Internet investments appear to be in. All of the money fed to the Internet start-ups by venture capitalists appears to have made the market for Internet products similar to the market for water with the resulting output of Internet companies overwhelming the demand. This appears to be true for e-commerce companies, although many of their business models were questionable. It is difficult to know for sure whether the poor profits are due mainly to overinvestment in a market that was feasible or whether they are the result of the reckless atmosphere of granting funds to untested, inexperienced individuals with ideas that were poorly thought out and for whom zero was the proper amount of investment.

Overinvestment appears to have decimated telecom companies such as Nortel and JDS Uniphase and damaged the seemingly invincible Cisco. Overcapacity has led to some remarkable balance-sheet losses. In these latter cases, unlike the former, it is clear that their business models worked. Overinvestment is a short-term phenomenon, and we can expect these companies, or their replacements, to become long-term players in these markets.

The short-term future of other Internet markets is likely to be hit and miss. Chapter 4 listed characteristics that should lead to successful business models on the Internet. We will surely see the Internet used to transmit all forms of digital information. The music industry will find the Internet to be a very efficient mechanism, although it have an entirely different set of problems that are discussed in detail in chapter 7. Other Internet sites will switch away from advertising to more subscription-based models, as discussed in Chapter 6.

Broadband is coming, but quite slowly. Business models that depend on wide-scale broadband usage are likely to have to wait for a longer term, measured in decades as opposed to a year or two. Think of digital television as an analogy.

The seeming ease of entry into Internet businesses does not bode well for long-term profitability. The idea was that consumers would find it easy to comparison shop on the Web, using bots or just manual searches. The presumption was that Web sites would have to match the lowest price and that profits in this world would be hard to come by. This scenario is very close to what economists have in their model of competition, and a zero economic profit is the predicted outcome.

So far, this doesn't seem to be coming true. Consumers seem to have a surprisingly high degree of loyalty to the Web sites they use. Perhaps there will be the opportunity for some companies to generate long-run above-normal profits if they can create enough loyalty. That remains to be seen, however. It is still difficult to imagine that competition on the Internet will not be at least as intense as it is in the bricks-and-mortar world, and that doesn't bode well for Internet profits. For those who believe that lower costs will allow Internet companies to generate above-normal profits, the next section is the prescribed antidote.

Margins and Profits on the Net

In the long run, virtual stores have certain advantages and disadvantages relative to bricks-and-mortar retailers. The main advantage—the lack of physical storefronts—should translate into lower costs. It has often been presumed that these lower costs will translate into above-normal profit margins for a lengthy period of time.

In fact, these lower costs, presuming that they materialize, will lead to lower margins, at least in a long-run competitive environment. Even Internet skeptics, such as the Perkins brothers, authors of the *Internet Bubble,* did not realize that the margins will be smaller for the online versions of retailing businesses as compared to their bricks-and-mortar counterparts.[16] In their book, they tried to estimate reasonable profits for Internet companies by multiplying the (projected) revenues by the margin on sales found in the bricks-and-mortar equivalents to the Internet company.

Proper estimation of the profit margin on sales is required for any investors wishing to calculate the proper value of Internet companies based on projected sales as well as for companies trying to evaluate the contributions to the bottom line from their new Internet subsidiaries. Yet it appears to be the case that, like the Perkins brothers, most Internet analysts have overestimated margins on sales for several reasons.

First, there is a general misunderstanding about margins and about the relationship between margins and return on investment. As a purely accounting matter, industry margins will tend to fall as costs fall, which is the opposite of what is often assumed. Second, although it is true that a company that can reduce its costs will generally increase its return on investment, its returns will not increase if all competing companies also experience similar reductions in cost.

Understanding Profit Margins

My claim that industries with lower costs will also have lower margins may seem somewhat counterintuitive, at least at first.

The cause of the low profit margins is the fact that the Internet can reduce the cost of doing business. Wall Street analysts in the halcyon days of Internet investing (R.I.P. 1997–1999) liked to drool over Internet start-ups because they believed that virtual storefronts would be less expensive then creating real storefronts. Virtual storefronts do not require real estate, plumbing, show-rooms, dressing rooms, heating, or air conditioning. Virtual storefronts can be scaled up without having to hire additional em-ployees in many different locations. Virtual storefronts should be less expensive.

Of course, barebones warehouses are also less expensive than elaborate showrooms, and yet many products—automobiles, clothing, furniture, jewelry, and many others—are often sold in establishments that are not anything like a barebones warehouse. Cost minimization is not the same as profit maximization. Con-sumers often value the ambience and/or extra consideration that they are given in expensive retail establishments. When they do, barebones outlets, although they might have lower costs, are not going to be a more efficient or more successful form of retailing. The nature of the retailing has to match the tastes of consumers, a point I hope to have hammered home in Chapter 4.

Let us assume, however, that Internet retailing matches the tastes of consumers for some product categories and that Internet retailers have lower costs than their bricks-and-mortar counter-parts. What does that imply about profits?

It is useful to spend a little bit of time talking about profit margins. There is an important definitional concern that needs to be made right off the bat. Profit margins measure the rate of return on sales. This is quite different from the rate of return on invest-ment, which is often called the profit rate.

More generally, if companies in industry A have a smaller in-vestment relative to sales than do companies in industry B, then, for a similar level of competitiveness, the margin on sales will be smaller for companies in industry A. It is also the case that compa-nies in industry A have a smaller value-added.

This is illustrated in table 5-1, which represents three typical companies that are each in one of three different industries. Each industry is assumed to be competitive, implying that companies earn "normal" returns on their investments, assumed in the table to be 10 percent. The average company in industry A, labeled as "high investment," invests $150 million to generate yearly sales of $100 million. The typical company in industry B, labeled "medium investment," invests $100 million and generates yearly sales of $100 million. The typical company in industry C, labeled "low investment," invests $50 million to generate sales of $100 million.

The assumption that the industries are each competitive, and that each earns a normal (10 percent) return on investment implies that the low investment company generates $5 million in profit, the medium investment company generates $10 million, and the high investment company generates $15 million.

If the profit rate on investment were calculated, it would be 10 percent in each case, by construction. In spite of the fact that each company is equally profitable in terms of investment, the margin on sales, our prime focus here, is calculated in the last column. The high investment company has a margin of 15 percent, the medium investment company has a margin of 10 percent, and the low investment company has a margin of 5 percent.

What is going on? Simply put, sales margins are poor measures of profitability. Economists have known for a very long time that the use of sales margins can be quite misleading if one wishes to determine relative levels of profitability across industries.[17] Industries differ in the amount of investment needed to generate a dollar in sales. One of the important determining factors is

Table 5.1.

	Sales	Investment	Normal Profit	Margin on Sales
High Investment	$100,000,000	$150,000,000	$15,000,000	15.0%
Medium	$100,000,000	$100,000,000	$10,000,000	10.0%
Low Investment	$100,000,000	$50,000,000	$5,000,000	5.0%

whether the industry is at the beginning or the end of the production/distribution chain. Companies at the end of the chain often put very little of the value into the products they are selling and then generate very small returns on sales since they have very low investments per dollar of sales.

Grocery chains are famous for their low margins, generating only pennies on the dollar. So are dry goods retailers. The leading grocery store chains, such as Albertson's and Kroger's, generate margins on sales of between one and two percent, which are extremely low compared to most other companies and industries. Even the enormously successful Wal-Mart has a profit margin on sales of less than 3 percent. Companies in industries that have small value-added often trumpet this fact to demonstrate how competitive their market is, playing on the common misconception that margins on sales bear some relationship to the degree of competition.

Of course, the low margins in the grocery industry have nothing to do with any extra competitiveness in the grocery industry but are due instead to the low value-added per dollar of sales. The restaurant business, for example, has historically been at least as competitive, with new entrants dying in droves, yet the margin on sales for the typical restaurant is often five to ten times as high as that for the typical grocery store.[18] The grocery business distributes products after others have already created most of the value, whereas restaurants themselves create much of the value of their products. Economic theory correctly predicts that the markups and margins will be smaller for Albertson's and Kroger's than for McDonald's and Wendy's.

What does this discourse on profit margins have to do with Internet companies? Most analysts have assumed that, because companies doing business on the Net will have lower costs, this will translate into the ability to generate higher investment returns and higher margins than their bricks-and-mortar counterparts. At one level this seems to make sense. After all, everything else being equal, companies that have managed to achieve a cost advantage over their competitors *in the same industry* do earn higher profits and margins than their higher-cost competitors.

But as we have seen, *margins* are significantly related to value-added and investment per dollar of sales. If Internet companies actually have lower costs, then they also will have lower investment required per dollar of sales, which should be expected to translate into lower margins if competition drives investment returns to normal levels. On the other hand, if Internet companies were to have higher returns on investment, this should help increase profit margins. I will discuss returns on investment in the next section.

Low margins for Internet companies do not mean that they are poor investments. Just as it would be a mistake to presume that supermarkets or other retailers with little value-added (e.g., Wal-Mart) were bad investments, one should not assume that Internet companies with low margins are necessarily bad investments.

The cautionary tale, however, is that, when estimating future profits for Internet businesses, one should use lower margins than for similar bricks-and-mortar companies. Buyers shouldn't get suckered by the claims to the contrary. Otherwise, companies will overpay when calculating the value of Internet properties, whether stocks or entire businesses, or they might overestimate the benefit to their bottom line if their Internet business is developed in-house.

The Nature of Competition in Internet Markets

Unrestricted competition, as I have already pointed out, tends to force profitability to levels just barely adequate to justify the investments that were made. Naturally, this would also lower profit margins from levels that might be achieved in a less competitive market.

In the previous section, I demonstrated that, for any level of competition, decreases in cost would result in lower profit margins on sales, assuming that profit rates on investment remain constant. In this section I examine the assumption that returns on investment in Internet-based businesses will be the same as in the bricks-and-mortar versions of those industries.

Economists consider markets competitive when easy entry keeps the typical company in the industry earning only normal returns on investment—in other words, returns unimpressive enough to keep potential entrants uninterested. In less competitive industries, i.e., those where entry is more difficult, even average companies can earn above-normal returns on investment.

If all the companies in a competitive industry achieve a reduction in costs, their profits, after an initial and temporary rise, will return to normal when new capacity and new entrants suck up any excess profits. Memory chip manufacturers, for example, constantly have falling costs, but new investment in fabrication plants at every uptick in profits eventually pushes profits back to the low levels that plague very competitive industries.

These are the standard textbook results for competitive industries. How do we know this model of competition is not just some aberrant creation from professors too long ensconced in their ivory towers? Because there is overwhelming evidence accumulated over the years to support many of its implications, which is available in many microeconomics texts.

If Internet retailers have lower costs than bricks-and-mortar retailers, there are two possible long-term outcomes (in each I assume that the stores on the Net will have lower margins than current bricks-and-mortar companies). The key to the profitability of these Internet-based industries, relative to their bricks-and-mortar counterparts, depends on whether Internet-based companies will compete mainly against the bricks-and-mortar companies in the same general business, or whether they will compete mainly against other Internet-based companies.

In many instances, bricks-and-mortar retailers will coexist side-by-side with online retailers, just as mail-order companies have coexisted with bricks-and-mortar retailers. That is because consumers will segment themselves into those who prefer virtual and those who prefer bricks-and-mortar retailing. In this case, the cost advantage of online retailers over bricks-and-mortar retailers is largely irrelevant for profitability, just as discount houses are not necessarily more profitable than full-service providers. Competition in each segment will occur largely between companies in a segment, just as convenience stores compete largely with other convenience stores and supermarkets with other supermarkets. Assuming that each market is competitive, every drop of excess profit will be squeezed out of the market for the typical company in each segment. That means that the investment returns will be similar in both, but since the investment per dollar of sales is lower for Internet companies, so too is their average margin on sales, as explained in the previous section.

In other instances, Internet-based companies and bricks-and-mortar companies might be considered perfect substitutes for one another; for example, consumers might have absolutely no preference between buying a book online and buying a book in a physical store. If Internet companies have lower costs, all the bricks-and-mortar booksellers will be driven out of business by the more efficient Internet sellers, just as horses and buggies were driven out of business by automobiles. This might take a while, but eventually the industry would consist only of Internet booksellers. Of course, the opposite would be true if Internet companies had higher costs. While the transition was occurring, bricks-and-mortar companies would be earning below-normal profits, and Internet companies might be earning above-normal profits. But after the Internet companies had vanquished the bricks-and-mortar companies, profits for the Internet companies would return to a normal level. Note, however, that the newer, more efficient industry, now comprised of Internet companies, will have lower margins on sales than the old industry did before the advent of competition with the Internet companies.

And of course, in some instances, Internet companies will find that they do not belong in an industry—for example, selling dog food over the Internet—and they will go out of business and not be replaced by other Internet companies.

This is not to say that some Internet retailers will not have higher returns than others. There is always some variation in performance, and even in competitive industries, some companies earn above-normal returns. It is a simplification of the competitive model that variations in profits are often assumed away, and it is a mistake to take those economic models too literally. Companies that have figured out how to give consumers the most bang for the buck, how to lower their costs below those of other companies *in their industry,* or how to find a niche that is difficult for potential competitors to imitate will earn above-normal returns, as has always been the case.

Notes

1. In the economics literature, as can be verified in virtually any microeconomics textbook, the surpluses are called "consumer's surplus" and "producer's surplus."

2. The surplus received by producers is related to profits but is not necessarily the same as profits. Without going through the distinctions between long run and short run I cannot fully explain how they might differ. It might be best to just say that in the long run, when companies have the option of exiting the industry, their surplus is equal to profit. In the short run, when there is a temporary imbalance or when companies have insufficient time to exit the industry, the company generates surplus if it can more than cover its variable costs, i.e., the costs that change when output changes.

3. Or, advertisers get less of the audience than they would like, causing advertising rates to be higher.

4. This is being copyedited just after the fourth quarter results in 2001 have been released. Amazon reported positive accounting profits for the first time (accounting profits are always higher than economic

profits, since economic profits only exist if the return is higher than average). Most estimates for the future still predict negative profits, and only time will tell whether Amazon is actually capable of sustaining profits.

5. This point is, of course, neither shocking nor new, but it has been largely ignored in the current discussions about the Internet economy. As the entrails of the Internet stock market bust are more carefully analyzed, the realization of the possibility of overinvestment will become more common. But questions about the level of investment should have been heard earlier, and the difficulty of overinvestment is always possible, not just for the Internet.

6. There are several sites that list the casualties of the Internet meltdown, but I find the most colorful to be at *http://fuckedcompany. com/hof/*.

7. Unless one believes a result of the "network externality" literature that the market cannot coordinate the behavior of consumers, leading to either excess inertia or excess momentum (excessively rapid or excessively slow adoption of products and technologies). I discuss this literature in Chapter 3 and present, in part, my critique (with Margolis) of this research.

8. Once it is understood how markets work, it becomes clear that certain attempts to equalize wages across occupations, a movement known as "comparable worth" that is thought to provide similar wages for similar "value," are misguided and inefficient.

9. Food can also be used as an example since, even though world population continues to increase to unprecedented levels, food production capacity continues to outstrip it, and prices fall along with profits. That is why there is less land devoted to farms, and the government has had to step in and try to artificially restrict output so as to increase the profits of farmers.

10. This assumption is normally included so that the demand curves facing individual companies can be drawn as a horizontal line.

11. It is incorrect to call a copyright a "monopoly" since it doesn't, by itself, restrict competition from other authors producing substitute products.

12. Redistribution in markets is most often not a zero-sum game, meaning that policies that enrich either consumers or producers do not leave the total the same but most often reduce the amount that is split between the two groups. The gain to taxicab owners is actually less than the loss to consumers, and it is this element of the policy that economists most object to.

13. This figure comes from Jim Lesczynski "Follow that cab . . . to oppression," March 19, 2001, available at *http://www.liberzine.com/ jimlesczynski/010319nytaxis.htm*.

14. Sometimes, domestic restrictions can benefit companies with products that are imported into the United States. To protect domestic producers, the U.S. government restricted Japanese automobile imports in the 1980s. The Japanese producers discovered that, by using their government to determine which automobiles could be imported into the United States to meet the U.S. restrictions, they could limit competition among themselves, raising their prices and profits on automobiles sold in the United States. When the U.S. government was willing to drop the restrictions, the Japanese producers voluntarily continued the restrictions. "Throw us in the briar patch," they said.

15. See the interesting paper by Solveig Singleton "Will the Net Turn Car Dealers into Dinosaurs? State Limits on Auto Sales Online" Cato Briefing Paper, July 25, 2000, at *http://www.cato.org/pubs/briefs/ bp58.pdf*.

16. Anthony Perkins and Michael Perkins, *The Internet Bubble*. (New York: Harper Business, 1999). On page 243 they state: "We have assumed that as the Internet becomes more established, competition will drive net margins to become aligned with those of more traditional companies in similar subsegments." Since they realize that margins are related to value-added, their assumption may just reflect

a belief that Internet companies will not have cost advantages over bricks-and-mortar companies.

17. For example, see my paper "On the Measurement and Mismeasurement of Monopoly Power," *International Review of Law And Economics,* vol. 7, June 1987, pp. 89–99.

18. Albertson's and Kroger's, two large supermarket chains, have margins on sales that averaged between one and two percent for the period 1996–2000. Retailers such as K-mart and Wal-mart averaged between .4 percent and 3 percent respectively. Macdonald's and Wendy's averaged 14 and 7 percent respectively. There is little doubt that Wal-Mart was more successful than Wendy's over this period, but the value-added differential swamped the other differentials. I could have chosen other industries with much higher margins, but these are all retailers to the public.

Chapter 6

Can Advertising Revenues Support the Net?

There has been a movement away from subscription revenues and toward pure advertising as the basis for supporting many Internet Web sites. This business model, mimicking over-the-air television, has many flaws that will become apparent as this market matures. Subscriptions are going to come back, in part because advertising revenues do not have much leeway for further growth, and most sites will need subscriptions to support their content.

The online world was originally a subscription-based world. Users of the leading online services, CompuServe, Genie, and AOL, did not encounter advertising to any real extent. Users paid their fixed monthly fee, which usually included five or so hours of use, any additional charges brought about by usage of the system that exceeded the five-hour limit, and sometimes additional fees for using a portion of the service that was considered a premium area, such as getting old newspaper stories. This was how online services generated their revenues. There was very little advertising.

The exception to this story was Prodigy. This service, owned jointly by Sears and IBM, was ahead of its time. Unlike the others, it charged a flat monthly rate for unlimited connection time during the early and mid-1990s. Prodigy also had notoriously ugly graphic advertisements scattered throughout its site. The advertisements and other aspects of the site were the object of scorn among more knowledgeable computer users who often mocked the novice users attracted to Prodigy. Nevertheless, thanks to its flat fee structure, Prodigy became the leading online service in the mid-1990s.

By including advertising and removing hourly fees, two trends that were later adopted by all of the online services, Prodigy showed itself to be ahead of its time—probably too far ahead. Although Prodigy achieved the highest market share of any online service under its unlimited-use pricing plan, Prodigy itself was not profitable. Its owners therefore decided to switch to a pricing scheme similar to those of its competitors.

With its pricing advantage gone, consumers rapidly shifted their allegiances, and the primary winner was the online service that had been winning the majority of independent reviews—AOL.[1] A few years later, all of the major online services, led by AOL, began charging a flat monthly fee for unlimited usage and also began putting more advertising on their sites.

With the advent of the Internet, many Web sites tried to emulate the early subscription-based model used by the online services. The *Wall Street Journal, Slate,* ESPN Sports, and others attempted to charge users for accessing the material on their sites. This was not to last, however.

Perhaps wishing to keep information from feeling bad or claustrophobic, since pundits such as Kevin Kelly, in his *New Rules for a New Economy*, mentioned in Chapter 3, argued that information wanted to be free, many Internet sites decided to forgo subscription revenues.

After succumbing to the will of freedom-hungry information, the route these Internet sites took was one that is quite familiar to anyone who has watched broadcast television, which is just about everyone. That route is one that tries to maximize audience size so as to maximize advertising revenues.

Currently, the market appears to have rejected subscription

fees. Many of the content providers that had tried subscription fees (*Slate*, TheStreet, Microsoft Investor) have reverted to covering their costs through advertising revenues alone. The co-founder of TheStreet, a stock market site, is quoted as saying "Going free for news is a must if we are to compete world-wide for readers."[2]

Yahoo led the way in giving away information to maximize audience and advertising revenues. A consumer going to its Web site could get free news, including sports and business news. That is something that had previously cost money. Yahoo was paying for this service but giving it away to consumers. A consumer going to its site could also get free stock market quotes and stock market research tools. These had also previously cost consumers money. Consumers could get free e-mail. Free instant messaging. Free on-line communities. Free maps.

Yahoo, following this pure advertising model, became one of the great success stories. Its market capitalization grew like Jack's beanstalk, reaching just north of $200 billion in January of 2000. As a comparison, Viacom purchased CBS Inc. for $35 billion in the fall of 1999, and Walt Disney, a firm that has much more than its ownership of ABC, had a market capitalization of $70 billion at that time.[3] So, in principle, Yahoo could have purchased all three television networks and had change left over—and these values came entirely from an advertising-based model. I lost a lot of money betting that Yahoo was overpriced during the large run-up in its price. Although its later decline was a victory of sense over nonsense, it provided me with only small satisfaction that in no way balanced the losses I incurred as the stock rode upward.[4]

Many other companies adopted the Yahoo model and gave away lots of services for free. Free Web hosting. Free backup space. Free message boards. Free income-tax software. Even free Internet access and free computers.[5] Open an online brokerage account and you got paid $400 (E*TRADE). Information must have been very happy with all this freedom. In fact, many Web sites charged negative prices, meaning that they were paying consumers to come to their Web sites through promotions and give-aways.[6]

But an advertising-based model never made sense and was never going to generate sufficient value for all the Internet sites that intended to use it as their sole source of revenues.

The Inadequacy of the Television Model

Neither the pure subscription nor the pure advertising model makes as much sense as a hybrid model combining both subscriptions and advertising. Migrating the television model to the Internet seemed to make sense since both were expected to be mass media attracting large numbers of eyeballs.

But the mistake that was made was the opposite of the problem that sellers of online groceries made. Online grocers had too *little* regard for the habits and customs that had evolved slowly over time in the competitive marketplace. In the use of advertising as the sole support of content, the television model was accorded too *much* respect.

The television-advertising model is not one that had survived brutal competition with truly competitive alternatives. There is no doubt that television advertising was and is big business. At one time, ownership of a television station was considered tantamount to being given the right to print money, which is a testament to how profitable television was.

But the profitability did not come from the superiority of its revenue model. Instead, it came from the fact that television was an industry with limited entry. Creation and ownership of television stations was restricted by the government and by the limitations in the available television frequency spectrum. The result was that the number of licenses granted was far less than the level that might have reduced the profitability of television stations to a more normal level.[7]

More importantly, television stations did not have the option of using other models of revenue generation. Over-the-air broadcasts were available to anyone with an antenna and a television, making it impossible for television broadcasters to charge viewers even if the broadcasters had wanted to use a subscription-based revenue model.[8]

Advertising-based television, although a successful business, could not credit its success to its revenue-generation model. There was no Darwinian selection of the fittest—at least not until cable television entered the scene. Cable television, which is a hybrid of advertising and subscription, provides a degree of competition between different revenue models. And cable is at a disadvantage because not as many homes are passed by cable as are passed by broadcast signals. The current competition allows television viewers and the market to chose between different models. I do not believe that the final verdict is in, although I have elsewhere predicted that broadcast television would eventually lose its lead over cable due to cable's superior revenue-generation possibilities.[9] I still believe that over-the-air broadcasters, because of their reliance on an inferior revenue model, are doomed to eventually showing little more than old reruns, something of a role-reversal from the traditional relationship between cable and over-the-air broadcasters.

A somewhat different market, which has allowed various revenue-generation models to compete in a Darwinian fashion, is the magazine and newspaper market. Magazines can be entirely subscription-based or entirely advertising-based or a hybrid of the two. Any casual examination of this market clearly reveals that it is the hybrid model that dominates.

A combination of subscription and advertising revenues seems likely to replace pure advertising as the revenue model on the Internet because a dual revenue system has many advantages. Except for the television market, which is constrained, it is hard to find any other markets that choose to survive entirely on advertising alone. And as I have stated before, the past provides important information about the future. Always.

Advertising Effectiveness on the Internet

It is also unlikely that advertising revenue could be sufficient to support all the sites counting on it. First, the audience (measured in total viewing-hours) is not large compared to that of television, nor is it likely to be terribly large until television migrates to the Net. Current estimates of time spent on the Web average thirty minutes per day compared to four hours for television viewing, and more people watch television than use the Internet.

Second, Internet advertising will remain less effective than television advertising as long as it is so easy to avoid. If it becomes intrusive, not allowing the Internet user to move forward until the ad is viewed, there will likely be a backlash from users. But this intrusiveness is required to make the advertising more effective for those users who remain to encounter it.

Third, advertising budgets are not terribly malleable, and Internet advertising will have to come largely at the expense of other media. Taking away shares from other media will become increasingly difficult. Although Internet advertising is very good at segmenting the population according to tastes, these "narrowcast" messages will be insufficient to support mainstream content.

Let's take these points one at a time.

Size of Audience

Television is a passive form of entertainment and is by far the leading recreational activity among Americans. The typical household spends over seven hours a day watching television and adults spend approximately four-and-a-half hours each in front of the set.[10] Televisions are virtually ubiquitous in the United States, with households more likely to have televisions than telephones. Another leading recreational activity is listening to music, often on the radio, and this too is a passive activity.

The Internet has been very successful in drawing many users into more activities that are not passive or that are at least far less passive. It is unclear that these activities will permeate society the way television viewing has. Further, many households and individuals do not own computers and are unlikely to find a computer a particularly compelling purchase. Non-computer Internet devices have been duds in the market, and are likely to remain so until and unless streaming video and music are able to replace television and radio. This is not about to happen anytime soon.

The average time spent by Americans on various activities in the year 2000 is represented in Figure 6.1.

Figure 6.1. Hours per Person in 2000

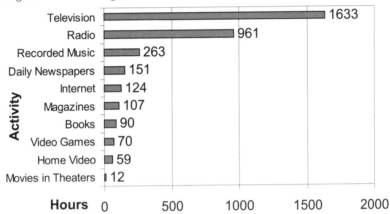

Source of data: Veronis, Suhler.

Clearly, the Internet has a long way to go before it can be considered to be in the same league as radio or television. The only non-passive activities on the list are video games and the Internet. Recorded music and home video require that the user chooses the CDs or tapes, but this is hardly more active than changing a channel with a remote control device.

Now it is true that other non-passive leisure activities such as sports participation are not listed here, but these activities would also be dwarfed by television viewing.

Advertising Effectiveness on the Net

One of the reasons that television advertising has been effective is that it is very difficult to avoid. Television advertisements are strategically placed to maximize the likelihood that viewers are engrossed in the programming and will thus be most likely to see the advertisement. These advertisements are often placed just before an important point in the program. Viewers who change channels or leave the room do so at their peril, for they may misjudge the time and miss the denouement of the program they have been watching for the last fifty minutes.

Television viewers are used to these intrusions and understand that they are a necessary evil if they are to see the free programming. Internet users are not used to them, and it is unclear what they would do if advertisements on the Internet were to mimic their television brethren. Understand what that would mean. To effectively mimic how television does it, Internet advertisements would take over the entire screen for a minute or two and prevent the user from doing anything else on the Internet (or on the computer). It is unclear whether this is even technologically feasible. There are some programs that require an advertisement to always be present, but this is not the same as preventing other uses of the computer. (It is hard to imagine how a program could take over the entire computer, and I am not sure if there is any way to control the browser to keep the user from moving forward.)

A more recent style of advertisement that has generated a great deal of press is the "pop-under" advertisement, with the best known being the little X-10 hidden camera, that, if you can believe the innuendo in the advertising, would allow the purchaser to take pictures of scantily clad young women if only he can lure them into the room with the hidden camera. This advertisement appears in a new window that pops up behind the main browser window. There are mixed opinions about the effectiveness of these advertisements, with some claiming that the level of annoyance is such that it will be harmful to the advertiser.[11] In fact, this more intrusive level of advertising is more like television.

Pop-under advertising is still far less intrusive than pop-over, or multiple pop-overs. Anyone who has accidentally encountered an Internet porn or warez site (and who reading this book would admit to going to these sites intentionally?) has seen a form of advertising that is extremely difficult to get rid of. Numerous windows open up all over the screen, each advertising a different site. Attempts to close these windows often lead to new windows popping up on the page. You practically have to fight with your PC to get control over the screen. This very annoying advertising is an example of what Internet advertisers could do if they really wanted to make sure the user was unable to avoid the advertisements. Porn advertisers apparently believe that such advertising provides more benefit than harm. I suspect other advertisers will follow their lead without being quite so aggressive.[12]

Currently, however, advertisements on most Web sites are still largely of the fixed-banner variety. Click-through rates, which are the general form of measurement, have been falling fairly steadily over the last few years, evidence that banner advertising is increasingly ineffective at driving traffic to Web sites.[13] Click-throughs are measured as the percentage of individuals who actually click on a banner advertisement when visiting a Web page containing a banner ad.

The Internet Advertising Bureau has argued, contrary to what I have suggested above, that banner advertisements are indeed very effective at altering consumer perceptions and increasing sales, and that click-through rates are irrelevant. These results are contained in a study performed in 1997 (jointly with Millward Brown Interactive) that would appear to be scientifically rigorous.[14]

I find the results extremely hard to believe, however. For example, they report that Web surfers enjoyed banner advertising, with 26 percent of respondents stating that it was "great." They also report that Web surfers formed a more favorable opinion of a company if it advertised on the Web than if it didn't. I have trouble understanding why Web surfers would have this opinion, unless they thought of advertisers as partners helping to make their surfing possible—i.e., providing the funds for the low prices and giveaways that were the characteristics of early Internet commerce.

I think it is difficult to imagine television viewers harboring similar opinions of television advertisers because viewers have no doubt about the survival of the medium. In 1997, when the study was conducted, Web advertising was still in its infancy, and the future of the Web was unclear. Web surfers might have felt protective of its future, but I have trouble believing that most Internet users these days believe the advertising on the Web says very much about the firm doing it, or that it is "great" to have. Additionally, I believe there is a flaw in the experimental design that plays to this early audience's interest in trying to promote advertising on the Web.

In the main experimental component of the study, surfers were exposed to a single experimental banner advertisement without fully knowing that the advertisement was part of an experiment. These users were later asked a series of questions about the advertisement at various time periods up to a week after the exposure. Respondents reported considerable awareness of the banner advertisement from this one exposure, with little change in their extra awareness even a week later. I find this just too incredible to believe. What is not known from the experimental design is whether Web users were on extra alert when the experimental banner was served to them.

Little details are crucial in this experimental design. When users at particular sites clicked on a banner for "celebrity news," some people were randomly selected and asked to fill out a demographic survey. After completing the survey, users were fed the celebrity information page they had requested, and this page contained either a control banner advertisement or an experimental banner advertisement. Were there any hints in the survey that an experiment having to do with advertising might be taking place? The report doesn't make it clear, although it would be useful to know.

It would have been a better design to ask the respondents to fill out the survey after they had seen the page with experimental or control banner ads. That way their behavior toward the ads could not possibly have been tainted by the fact that they were taking a survey. This problem may well be responsible for the survey's findings.

Even so, the study's authors conclude that Internet advertisements are only slightly more effective than television advertising (20 percent) although somewhat less effective than print media. The Internet–TV differential is small enough that my later assumption that the two media are the same may not even be inconsistent with the findings.[15]

Advertising Budgets

Advertising effectiveness has long been one of the mysteries of business. It is quite clear that advertisers do not have a very good idea of how effective their advertising is in creating additional sales. This was forcefully driven home several years ago when "people meters" were first introduced.

People meters are devices that can measure how many individuals are watching a program and for how long they are watching it with a requirement that viewers click a button to register when they are viewing television. The typical audience-measuring device had previously been written surveys that random viewers filled out. When the results of people meters and surveys were compared, it was determined that people meters registered a smaller audience than did surveys.

The major television networks objected to the use of people meters, fearful that the smaller measured audience would lead to a decline in advertising revenues. And major advertisers indicated that if the television audience were smaller than they had previously thought, they would lower their advertising expenditures on television.[16]

Even if there were unanimity that people meters correctly measured audiences and that television audiences were smaller than previously thought, it would be irrelevant for advertising expenditures if advertisers had some good idea of how effective their advertising was. The logic is simple and compelling.

Assume an advertiser plans to purchase a one-minute television spot on a program such as *ER*. How much should he pay? The answer is that he should determine the extra profits that are generated by the additional sales resulting from the advertising; this is the maximum amount that should be paid.[17]

The people meter doesn't change the size of the *real* audience; it only indicates the size of the *measured* audience. If advertising expenditures were based upon the known effectiveness of advertising, switching to people meters would be irrelevant. Even if advertising budgets were based upon rules of thumb having to do with measured audience size, all of the rules would still hold, based on the old measurements that were used to derive those rules, and the switch to people meters would have merely required revising the rules, not the advertising budgets. Therefore, the brouhaha over the introduction of people meters is itself evidence that advertising budgets are not based on actual effectiveness.

Advertisers, therefore, operate largely in the dark with little in the way of hard data about how effective their advertising is.

Positive Aspects of Internet Advertising

One area where Internet advertising will shine is classified advertising, a very large advertising market of approximately $18 billion.[18] As discussed in chapter 4, classified advertising has large network effects and is a perfect form of advertising for the Internet. The eBay site can be thought of as the mother of these sites, but other specialized sites such as Hotjobs or Monster work the same way.[19]

Of course, whether consumers find the electronic version of classifieds easier to use is a function of their connection speed and the setup of the Web site. Also, local classified ads tend, at the moment, to favor print newspapers since the large number of non-

Internet users tends to give newspaper classifieds greater network effects than online classifieds might have. National classifieds (e.g., high-end employment possibilities) are therefore likely to migrate to the Internet before local classifieds.

Internet advertising of the banner variety does have some other advantages over other media such as television, radio, or magazines. One very important advantage, which sellers of Internet advertising are now trying to downplay, is the immediate feedback of advertising effectiveness through the measurement of click-through rates. Unlike other advertisements, banner advertisements don't just sit there. They are not completely passive. Banner advertisements actually do something when you click on them. This allows advertisers to gauge whether the audience is interested enough to actually follow through and try to get additional information. This is a very useful tool for advertisers.

The Internet Advertising Bureau, however, argues that click-through rates are unimportant. They argued this in 1997 when click-through rates were still high. They and others argue it even more forcefully now that click-through rates have fallen from above 5 percent in 1995 to under 0.5 percent in 2001.[20]

Another advantage of Internet advertising is its fine slicing and dicing of the audience, which allows great segmentation and the placement of ads catering to very narrow, specifically targeted groups. Magazines have a similar sort of targeting since they too appeal to very specific audiences. Television, radio, and newspapers, however, are not well suited to targeted advertising. The Internet is probably even more finely subdivided than magazines since Web pages are far more numerous than magazines. In principle, the Internet should be the king of targeting. The only problem is that these very small, very focused sites are not likely to have sophisticated advertising personnel, and advertisers may not find it as simple as they do in other, more professional, media to place ads where they want. This is a problem that has plagued cable television networks, which often have very small viewership.

Advertising Revenues on the Internet

It is difficult to know with any precision what the advertising revenues on the Internet are going to be. Nevertheless, given how effective one believes Internet advertising might be versus, for example, television, it is possible to put some benchmark estimates in place.[21]

Let's start with the television market. According to the Television Bureau of Advertising, total advertising revenue for cable and broadcast television was approximately $50 billion in 1999. What kind of comparisons can be made between television and the Internet?

First, we can examine the cost to an advertiser of an hour of the putative viewer's time. This is a somewhat unusual metric for comparing media, but one that I think can be informative.

The first row of Table 6.1 lists the average viewing time per user of the medium, about four hours for television and a half-hour for Internet use. The second column provides data for television, and the third column provides data for the Internet. All of the numbers for television are actual values, current as I write this. The bottom two numbers in the Internet column are hypothetical and are intended to make a point.

The second row provides the number of users, which is just about everyone for television, and about half the population for the Internet.[22] By multiplying the number of users by the number

Table 6.1. Advertising Cost Per Hour of Activity

	Television	Internet
1. Hours Viewing Media per Day	4	0.5
2. Size of Audience	265,000,000	132,500,000
3. Viewer-Hours per Day	1,060,000,000	66,250,000
4. Viewer-Hours per Year	386,900,000,000	24,181,250,000
5. Advertising Revenue	$50,000,000,000	$3,110,000,000
6. Price per Viewer-Hour	$0.129	$0.129

of hours per user we arrive at the number of viewer-hours per day in row 3. Row 4 multiplies this by 365 to get the yearly number of viewer-hours spent using each medium. Row 5 lists the advertising revenues for television but not the actual revenues for the Internet.[23] Instead, I calculate what the advertising revenues *should* be for the Internet given its audience size and assuming the same price per viewing hour for the two media. The logic of this is explained in the next few paragraphs.

The real question is whether the advertising value of an hour's contact with an Internet user is worth more or less than the value of an hour's contact with a television viewer. Television viewers are normally exposed to twelve to fifteen minutes of commercials in an hour. Internet users are exposed to any number of banner advertisements in an hour, depending on how many pages they view and how many advertisements are on those pages.

Given that television advertisements are more difficult to avoid, and given their greater audio-visual power, I very much doubt that advertisers would find the contact with an Internet user to be as valuable as the same duration of contact with a television viewer. Of course, Internet boosters would dispute this, and I have to admit that my view is not much more than a gut-level reaction although I like to believe that it is an informed gut-level reaction.

If we assume for the moment that the two media are, in fact, equally effective at influencing consumers given an hour's use of the medium, we arrive at an estimate of Internet revenues that would put it at parity with television. We merely multiply the number of Internet viewer-hours by the value of the viewer-hour in the television market. From the table above, that calculation turns out to be $3.1 billion.

On the basis of this table, the $3 billion figure above is about the maximum that could be expected. Even if Internet use were to double or triple, advertising revenues would seem unlikely to surpass the $10 billion level.

What are current Internet advertising revenues?

Although they are in a slump as I write this book, they appeared to be in the vicinity of $8 billion in 2000.[24] Estimates for 2001, based on part-year results, indicate that advertising revenues have fallen, perhaps into the range of $6 billion.[25] Some of this is classified advertising (5 to 10 percent), which I believe will do very well on the Internet.[26] Still, the advertising revenues generated would seem to already be on the high side. Some estimates are that revenues will double to $16 billion by 2005 although others see a more modest $10 billion.[27]

The $16 billion estimate is over four times the revenues that seem reasonable in the table above. In a relative sense, this implies that having a consumer using the Internet for an hour is four times as valuable as having a consumer watching television for an hour. One way to think of this is to imagine that television viewers watched four times as many advertisements as they now do, with an intensity equal to their current viewing. Since television advertising is currently near fifteen minutes an hour, increasing advertising intensity by a factor of four would be the equivalent of having the consumer watch nothing but ads.

Ignoring the question of why anyone would watch nothing but advertising, one needs to ask whether a viewer spending an hour watching one television ad after another is more or less valuable than a surfer exposed to current Internet pages for one hour. How much impact can advertising have in an hour, and is television such an ineffective medium that full-time television ad viewing is of less value to advertisers than part-time ad viewing on the Internet?

How could television, with its sound and moving pictures, be such an inferior medium? If current television advertising were so bad, would not television advertisers perhaps do better taking the lead from the Internet? Perhaps they should put fixed-banner ads with primitive animation and no sound on the television screen. Perhaps these banner ads should run for only a few seconds, and perhaps they should take up only part of the screen. This logic seems inescapable.

Obviously, I do not find this possibility plausible and thus conclude that current Internet advertising revenues appear to be too high relative to television advertising. It seems to be too high by a factor of at least two. Although the Internet is expected to grow, I think that Internet advertising will have trouble meeting these projections.

Of course, the astute reader might have noticed that I am assuming here that Internet advertising revenues will reflect the actual advertising values, whereas I explained earlier that advertisers often do not seem to know how effective their ads are. My assumption here that advertising revenues are related to real-world values seems to contradict my claim that advertising revenues have a life of their own that is independent of economic logic.

The reality is that, at some point, I expect advertisers to catch on to the fact that they are getting less bang for the buck in some media than in others and that there is some relationship between payback and advertisers' willingness to pay (just as they would have eventually realized that the people meter didn't really make a difference).

It should also be noted that in the year 2000, some advertising revenues were still coming from other Web sites with business models that have now been discredited because they ran out of money as the result of excessive expenditures on items like advertising. That is a major reason that the 2001 advertising revenues fell below the year 2000 levels.

Declining click-through rates, which are also likely harbingers of slow advertising growth to come, are obviously the result of both the clutter of multiple banners on a single page and the surfer's ability to screen them out while working. Doubling the number of advertisements should not double the revenues because each ad will be less effective than would have been the case with fewer advertisements.

Nor is the population of Internet users likely to grow rapidly. Most users with computers are already online. Those users without computers really are not likely to have much interest in Internet activities, as revealed by their lack of computers in the first place. As hard as it is for Internet devotees to believe, some people just don't care for interactive experiences. I suspect this is quite a large proportion of the population, including most senior citizens. That is why Internet devices, or Web appliances as they are more formally called, have been such failures. This will change, of course, when television is carried on the Internet.

The only serious route for advertising growth, then, would seem to be in the number of hours spent online. There is certainly room to grow from the current thirty to forty-five minutes per day.[28]

Without some major new activity, however, some sort of killer app, it is hard to know what will lead surfers to spend a great deal more time online. One hope that has been put forward is that the new generation of cell phones will push consumers to use the Internet. But this seems like another case of wishful thinking. The devices are too small to read, there is no keyboard, and there are few activities in which a phone is anywhere near as good a device as a computer. Phones are used by drivers, often to the chagrin of others. Drivers, we can fervently hope, will not be using the Internet.

It is also difficult to know where this extra time spent on the Internet will come from. The typical adult watches television four hours a day, listens to the radio two hours, sleeps eight hours, works eight hours, spends an hour with newspapers and magazines, and presumably spends some time on other activities such as eating dinner.

The bottom line? Internet advertising revenues are not likely to grow dramatically, if at all. They seem considerably higher now than they should be. For Web sites having difficulty making ends meet, their salvation is not likely to come from additional advertising revenues. Instead, they should test the water with small subscription fees and see if that can sustain them. Subscription fees are where the great revenue increases are likely to come from in the future. Indeed, they are where revenue increases are going to have to come from—if they come at all.

Notes

1. For a more detailed history of these online services, including product reviews, see my book with Stephen Margolis, *Winners, Losers & Microsoft*, Independent Institute, Oakland, CA, 2001, pp. 223–227.

2. See "Online Publisher TheStreet.com Plans to Drop Fees for Main Site," *Wall Street Journal* (online version), January 10, 2000.

3. See *http://204.202.137.115/sections/business/DailyNews/cbs_viacom_chronology_990907.html.*

4. As I write this, Yahoo has a market capitalization of approximately $10 billion, which still seems rather lofty to me.

5. Juno, among others, gave away free Internet service. PeoplePC gave away free computers, and TurboTax provided free software if you used its Web site instead of putting the software on your personal computer.

6. See, for example, Jennifer Mack, "The great Net giveaway gimmick: Call it promotion. Call it bribery. Increasingly, Web sites are using sweepstakes to attract an audience. Is the tactic working?" *ZDNet News*, October 24, 1999. *http://zdnet.com.com/2100-11-516015.html?legacy=zdnn.*

7. This is a very well accepted view among economists who have looked at the sale of television licenses. In general, a piece of paper, otherwise known as a license, will not have a positive price if it merely allows the owner to participate in a market that is fully competitive. This is the taxi-cab medallion story in a different guise. Think of it this way. Assume that all of the banks in your city were paying 5 percent interest on checking accounts. A new bank opens up and requires that you pay a yearly license fee to join the bank and earn the right to get 5 percent on your checking account. No consum-

ers would pay the yearly fee. If, on the other hand, the bank were to pay 8 percent—3 percent above market—then it could charge a fee that consumers would be willing to pay.

8. If the government had altered the laws somewhat, this might not have been so. In Great Britain, potential viewers were not allowed to view television programs without paying a yearly license fee. This was awkwardly enforced by using trucks with electronic eavesdropping devices that attempted to ferret out users who were watching television and not paying their license fees.

9. In a report conducted for CBS in 1990, I predicted that cable networks would overtake over-the-air broadcasters in terms of quality of programming, due to their superior revenue-generating ability. Specifically, I argued that over-the-air broadcasters would eventually show old reruns and that the quality original programming would appear on cable networks, the reverse of what was then the standard. We have come a long way toward the fulfilling of that prediction with more and more first-run programming appearing on cable (e.g., *The Sopranos*) and over-the-air broadcasters losing more and more market share.

10. The number in 2000 was seven hours and thirty-five minutes for households. See Nielsen media research, found on the TVB Web site *www.TVB.org*. The data for figure 6.1 also come from that site.

11. "Pop-Under Web Ads May Backfire, Says Jupiter," Reuters, July 26, 2001 at *http://www.thestandard.com/article/0,1902,28294,00.html*.

12. Some evidence that Internet sites are coming to this conclusion can be found in the *Wall Street Journal* article "Web Sites Ramp Up Ad Annoyances: More Deploy Ad 'Spawning,' to Increasing Irritation of Users" by Mylene Mangalindan, November 29, 2001.

13. The decline in click-through rates is well documented. See, for example, the "Reality Bytes" column in the July 23, 2001 *Wall Street Journal*, where it is claimed that rates are in the vicinity of .3 percent, less than a tenth of what they were in the mid 1990s.

14. See their 1997 Online Advertising Effectiveness Study, which argues that banner advertising is just the cat's meow. It can be found at *http://www.mbinteractive.com/site/iab/study.html.*

15. Of course, they are comparing a single banner advertisement to a single television advertisement, whereas I suggest comparing a viewer-hour of usage on each medium. This makes it very difficult to compare the two metrics.

16. Adam Snyder, "Trouble in Nielsenland; TV Shows Live or Die by Their Nielsen Ratings, but Television Executives Dispute Their Accuracy. At Stake: Billions of Dollars in Ad Revenues," *Newsday Magazine,* April 21, 1991, p. 8.

17. Somewhat more precisely, the advertiser should compare extra revenues net of variable costs, what economists call "quasi-rents." This would be approximated by EBID, earnings before interest and depreciation.

18. Newspaper advertising revenue is in the vicinity of $50 billion, and classified advertisements are estimated to be 33–40 percent of revenues.

19. Nevertheless, it is claimed that so far there is no diminution in newspaper classified revenues. In two studies, newspapers reported that their classified Web sites did not reduce their offline classified advertising revenues. This ignores the impact of outside sites, however. This was reported by Peter Zollman in "Are Newspapers Losing Revenue to Online Sites? Not Yet." *Newspapers and Technology,* June 2001, available at *http://www.newsandtech.com/issues/2001/06-01/ot/06-01_zollman.htm.*

20. In "Are Click-Through Rates Really Declining?" Jim Meskauskas claims that the rates were about 5 percent in 1997 and have fallen to about .5 percent recently. See Internet.com, January 16, 2001, at *http://clickz.com/cgi-bin/gt/article.html?article=3179.* See also "Three Years On: Ad and Click-Through Rates Decline," *Online Publishing*

News, February 24, 2000 at *http://www.onlinepublishingnews.com/ htm/n20000224a.htm.*

21. Note that these are advertisements by typical advertisers, not classified advertisements, which I expect the Internet to dominate at some point in the future.

22. There are supposedly 123 million Americans with Internet access, according to *Wow! Facts, 2001*—although I am somewhat loath to report facts from any publication with an exclamation point in the title. See *http://www.ewowfacts.com/wowfacts/chap47.html.* Nielsen/NetRatings puts the number of American Web users at 167 million in August of 2001. See *http://www.nielsen-netratings.com/ hot_of_the_net_i.htm.* The numbers used in the table are between these two estimates and are taken from the Television Bureau of Advertising.

23. Advertising revenues for television are for American broadcast and cable stations.

24. See "Net Ads Continue to Feel Signs of Economic Slowdown," dated April 23, 2001. The article, which can be found at *http://www. netads.com/articles/advertising/apr2001/003.html,* reports that the Internet Advertising Bureau logged $8.2 billion for U.S. Internet adverting in 2000. These data were for the United States only, and banner advertising had dropped to 40 percent. In "First Quarter Internet Ad Revs Soar," found in the August 8, 2000, issue of *InternetNews,* Josh Schonwald reported that Internet advertising revenues in the United States in the first quarter of 2000 were approximately $2 billion. This was before the Internet meltdown, and we know that much of this revenue came from advertisements placed by other Internet companies that later went belly-up. The article is at *http://www. internetnews.com/IAR/article/0,,12_432421,00.html.* A later article on ITP news by Mark Sutton, "Online Advertising Revenue Slips for the First Time," published on December 23, 2000, also claimed that despite a slowdown, 2000 was likely to hit $8 billion. This latter arti-

cle said that only half of the revenue was from banner advertising, however. See *http://www.itp.net/news/97756714361841.htm.*

25. Peter Loftus, "Weak Spending, Poor Ad Market to Hurt Results at Top Net Firms," *Wall Street Journal* (online version), July 10, 2001. However, a different projection by investment firm Veronis Suhler projects 2001 revenues at $7.5 billion and 2005 revenues at only $9.9 billion. See *http://www.msnbc.com/news/610170.asp.*

26. Other pundits have made similar projections. See, for example, "Journalism in a Digital Age" by Christopher Harper, who puts newspaper classified advertising at 40 percent of total newspaper advertising. See *http://media-in-transition.mit.edu/articles/harper. html.*

27. This projection was made for 2005 by Jupiter Communications, according to *Internet.com* in an article by Nancy Whiteman and Janet Ryan entitled "Internet Advertising in 2000 and Beyond ," December 18, 2000. See *http://www.clickz.com/article/cz.2994.html.*

28. Forty-five minutes according to the TVB Web site at *http://www.tvb. org/tvfacts/index.html.*

Chapter 7

Copyright and the Internet

Few subjects have caused as public and contentious a debate as the one that is now brewing over the digital reproduction and transmission of copyrighted materials. The ascendance and subsequent fall of Napster was the most visible aspect of this debate that is raging both in the halls of academe and in our legislative bodies. Yet the impact of copying has not been understood by many participants in this debate, and if the impact is not well understood, neither are any proposed solutions.

> For economic incentives to work appropriately, property rights must protect the rights of capital assets. . . . At present . . . severe economic damage [is being done] to the property rights of owners of copyrights in sound recordings and musical compositions . . . under present and emerging conditions, the industry simply has no out. . . . Unless something meaningful is done to respond to the . . . problem, the industry itself is at risk.
>
> Alan Greenspan[1]

The Internet is capable of altering the nature and degree of copying, appearing to threaten the very purpose of copyright and creating what appear to be unprecedented enforcement challenges. Although much of the recent focus has revolved around the Napster case (which is already beginning to recede from memory and may be largely forgotten by the time this book is published), the digitization of any artistic creation—whether audio, video, or the written word—threatens, or appears to threaten, current copyright regimes, as Napster's successors Bearshare, Limewire, AudioGalaxy, and Morpheus make clear.

It is unclear whether copyright can continue to provide ample incentives for artistic creation. Will authors be able to appropriate more or less of their works' value than they have in the past? How does digital storage change the balance between authorized and unauthorized use? What pricing schemes are likely to arise? What legal rules strike the best balance between consumptive efficiency and productive efficiency? That is, how do we maximize use and creation at the same time? These questions will form the focus of this rather lengthy chapter.

To keep things in perspective, we should remember that copying technologies have been in existence for several generations. Doom-and-gloom scenarios have been raised before, and copyright owners have seldom suffered great harm even when they were not given extra protection from copying technologies. Videocassette recorders are one example. Audiotaping, to which the Alan Greenspan quote refers, was another. How does the Internet change things?

The greatest threat to copyright owners has always come from organized, large-scale unauthorized copying. The digitizing of artistic works and the ubiquity of the Internet have brought with them the increasing potential to organize what would otherwise be unorganized, making pirating cheaper, easier, and more widespread than ever before. This is what makes the current copying crisis more significant than the "crises" of video- and audiotaping and should cause a serious examination of the issues even if the copyright owners have cried wolf often in the past, as history shows that they have.

For reasons explained in detail below, current pirating-distribution technologies appear capable of destroying the value of copyright (although the recording industry failed to present evidence of such an impact in the Napster case). There are two slightly different technologies now in use to transfer files among users. Both systems essentially allow individuals to access and download music (MP3) or other files that reside on the computers operated by other members of the system. These systems are called peer-to-peer systems since the files that are transferred are all stored on standard, non-commercial PCs. One type of system, such as Napster, uses a central server to act as an intermediary in searches for particular songs or files. The other type of system (pure peer-to-peer systems usually based on Gnutella, the first of these programs) forgoes the central server, allowing users to search for files (often audio, video, or software program files) on other computers and download these files at will. Although these seem like a pirate's dream, it is possible, in theory at least, that copyright owners might weather this new form of piracy in either of two ways.

First, it is possible that copyright harms can be ameliorated through the mechanism of "indirect appropriability" if several changes are put in place regarding the way these systems are used.[2] (Indirect appropriability is basically the idea that under certain conditions, copyright owners can collect for the unauthorized copying by charging higher prices for the originals.) Unfortunately for copyright holders, it would have been easier to convert a centrally organized system such as Napster into a more copyright-friendly system than it will be to convert the pure, dispersed peer-to-peer systems that appear to be replacing Napster. Thus the recent attempts by the record industry to shut down Napster may backfire by moving users to the more difficult to control pure peer-to-peer systems and may also harm the chances for appropriation of value on Napster or similar systems.

Second, the possibility of a copy-protection scheme known as digital rights management (DRM, also sometimes known as automated rights management or ARM) might also ameliorate copyright harms by making it much more difficult for unauthorized copies to be made in the first place. DRM works by inserting a code in the intellectual product that prevents copying some or all of the work without acquiring the rights through legitimate means, including the possibility of pay-as-you go pricing built into the product. These payments are sometimes known as micropayments since they can, in principle, be much finer than the all-or-nothing purchases that are typical of most physical manifestations of intellectual properties such as CDs and books. The specter of such self-enforcing copyright has caused alarm among groups of scholars and users who argue that it would give too much power to copyright owners and damage the current balance between producers and users. However, as I demonstrate below, there is little economic support for this concern. A review of the basic economics involved is a necessary starting point.

The Economic Impacts of Copying

The issue at the heart of copyright, indeed at the heart of all intellectual-property law, is the degree to which the copyright owner can appropriate the value produced by the consumption, or appreciation, of his or her work by others.[3]

The correct level of appropriation is at the center of many disputes, both current and historical. How much appropriation is the right amount?[4] Is it possible to have too much appropriation? What impact do technologies have on appropriation?

Economists have tended to focus on the trade-off between consumption efficiency (maximizing the amount consumers get of any produced intellectual product) and production efficiency (preserving incentives to create these products).[5] On the one hand, if the copyright holder could not appropriate any revenues from users, the creators of intellectual properties would be expected to produce too few intellectual products, probably far fewer than would be optimal.[6] On the other hand, by providing copyright owners some degree of control over the use of these products by restricting others' ability to make copies, consumption of these products is decreased from "ideal" levels. This restriction in use is sometimes carelessly referred to as a loss due to the "monopoly" of the copyright owner. As Edmund Kitch (a law professor at the University of Virginia who has written extensively on intellectual-property issues) correctly points out, providing property rights does not confer economic monopoly—which would imply that consumers have only a small number of alternative products that are not very good substitutes.[7] In reality, the "monopoly" conferred by copyright is no greater than the monopoly that each worker has on his efforts, or that each company has on products bearing its name. Still, monopoly power or not, the ideal number of reproductions of a public good—a public good being defined as a good that does not get used up when consumed, what is often called *nonrivalrous consumption*—would require a quantity of reproductions above the level that copyright owners would find in their best interest to produce, and thus too few reproductions would be created.[8]

Even if a technology were to increase the revenues of copyright owners, for example by increasing the pool of users, the relative level of appropriability might still be diminished. In terms of a simple analogy, if we increase the size of the pie, even a smaller share might lead to a piece that is of larger absolute value. In such a case, the copyright owner would still suffer harm compared to an instance where appropriability was kept constant (unless it were impossible to increase the size of the pie without also decreasing the share going to the copyright holder).[9] This distinction is relevant to discussion of the impact of technologies on the financial remuneration achieved by copyright holders.

Direct Economic Effects of Copying Technology

The pirating of copyrighted materials is normally thought to be harmful to the interests of copyright owners.[10] This is because piracy is often expected to prevent the copyright owner from appropriating any of the value created by the work, which goes instead to the users engaged in piracy. The mechanism by which unauthorized copying may harm the owners of intellectual products is straightforward enough that no detailed explanation seems necessary. Potential consumers are no longer compelled to purchase the product from the copyright owner when the option of using unauthorized copies is available to them. Defections from the legitimate market are normally expected to reduce the revenues that can be earned in the market.

In some instances, however, the impact of piracy on the copyright holder's ability to appropriate the value of the work will be negligible. One obvious instance is the case where the individual engaging in pirating would not have purchased an original even if pirating were not an option.[11] In this case, the prevention of piracy would provide no pecuniary reward for the copyright owner and would only diminish the gratification of the individual engaged in piracy.

A different situation in which copying might be helpful, or at least not harmful to copyright owners, is when piracy results in an "exposure effect"—a form of advertising or sampling that might ultimately lead to larger sales of legitimate versions.[12] For example, in the case of pirated software, users of pirated versions might find themselves wanting the manuals and technical support that would only be available to authorized users. Or, as claimed in the Napster defense, unauthorized Napster users may just sample songs to get a better idea of which CDs to buy.

A more recent claim is that copying may benefit copyright holders when network effects are strong.[13] An example of network effects for products prone to piracy might be word-processing software that becomes more valuable to a user the more other individuals are using the same word processor.[14] With more users, it becomes easier to exchange files with a greater number of people. In such an instance, it is conceivable that the extra value that paying customers receive from the larger user base, extra value that can be appropriated by the copyright owner, and which would be enhanced by users of pirated versions, might outweigh any revenues lost by the copyright holder as a result of being unable to prevent piracy. If the prevention of copying resulted in few former pirates paying full price, the prevention of unauthorized copying might prove financially harmful to the interests of the copyright owner. Of course, if all or enough of the pirates were to become purchasers of authorized versions when pirating was no longer possible, then the prevention of piracy would still be remunerative for the copyright owner even in the presence of network effects.

Even though, in a world characterized by either exposure effects or network effects, piracy might work to actually enhance the revenues of the copyright owner, it should be noted that appropriability is not necessarily enhanced. Both network and exposure effects increase the gross amount of the value received by consumers, allowing the copyright owner to generate more revenues with constant or even somewhat reduced levels of appropriability. In our pie analogy, the size of the piece might be increasing even if the piece's share of the whole were decreasing, as long as the pie itself were growing rapidly enough. So even if pirating were beneficial to copyright owners, meaning that the copyright owner received larger revenues (a larger absolute size of the pie), that doesn't mean that appropriability would be increasing or even constant. (The copyright owner's share of the now larger value generated by the intellectual product might be smaller.)

Of course, these are the exceptions to the more general rule that allowing potential consumers to pirate copies of a work is likely to reduce the revenues available to the copyright owner.

Indirect Economic Effects of Copying Technology

As noted, copyright owners are sometimes able to collect revenue from unauthorized copiers by charging higher prices for the originals from which the unauthorized copies are made, a result known as "indirect appropriability." The basic mechanism is simple: If the copyright owner knows which originals will be used to make copies, a higher price can be charged for them, allowing the copyright holder to capture part, all, or more of the revenue than might have been appropriated through ordinary sales if unauthorized copying could be prevented.

This can be made clear with a simple example. Assume that each and every purchaser of a compact disc makes a single audiocassette copy to play in their automobile. No one makes copies from borrowed CDs. Assume further that this copying, although illegal, is unstoppable. What would be the impact on the copyright holders who, in addition to selling compact discs, had also planned to sell prerecorded tapes?

Since each original CD will have a copy made from it, and since it is reasonable to infer that the consumers of originals place some value on the ability to make a copy, each consumer's willingness to pay for the original CD is higher than it would otherwise be. The copyright owner can capture some of this additional value by charging a higher price for the CD.[15] This is the basic idea behind indirect appropriability. The logic here is the same as it would be for any durable good that can be resold into another market. If automobiles could not be resold, for example, the price that consumers would be willing to pay for new autos would undoubtedly fall.

Whether the copyright owner is better off or worse off in a regime of unfettered copying depends on the particular circumstances. Assume, for example, that all consumers would be willing to pay nine dollars for a particular CD and would also be willing to pay four dollars for a cassette tape of the same music that they can play in their automobile cassette players (assume they do not have CD players in their automobiles). If home taping were allowed and consumers made cassettes, the sellers of CDs would discover that they could raise the price of CDs to thirteen dollars without any loss of sales (assuming zero cost for the cassette and the time to make the tape). If home taping were disallowed, under the same assumed circumstances the seller of prerecorded tapes could charge a price of four dollars and capture this group's value. In this case (where the costs of making cassettes is assumed to be zero), the seller would be unharmed by the copying and would therefore presumably be indifferent to whether copying was allowed or not.

If there are costs in making copies, whether the prevention of unauthorized taping is profit-enhancing or -decreasing will depend on the relative cost difference between individuals and firms in making and delivering copies. If it is much less expensive to make prerecorded cassettes commercially than to have them made one at a time at home, then it would be inefficient for personal copying to replace commercial production, and the copyright owner will not be able to net as much from the home-taping consumer (who deducts the cost of the blank cassette and his time from his willingness to pay) as he would from a sale of cassettes. Note, however, that costs include shipping, inventorying, and delivery to the consumer, not just manufacturing, so that the cost advantages of prerecorded tapes are at least questionable.

Another complicating possibility would arise if there were a subgroup of music listeners that purchases prerecorded tapes for the home instead of purchasing CDs. If the price that had been established for this group were also nine dollars, then the seller of prerecorded tapes would be in something of a bind in terms of capturing revenues from both groups of cassette listeners. If the price of prerecorded cassettes were lowered to four dollars to capture the value from the automobile cassette users, the seller would lose five dollars from those individuals who would be willing to pay nine dollars to purchase prerecorded tapes for home-listening. If the seller kept the price at nine dollars, he would make no sales to those wishing to listen to cassettes in automobiles.

In this case, allowing copying would benefit the copyright owner. Indirect appropriability would allow the seller to capture the four dollars from CD purchasers by raising the price of CDs to thirteen dollars, and the seller could still collect the full nine dollars from those who buy prerecorded tapes for the home. (The assumption that no copies are made from borrowed CDs is still in place.) In this instance, allowing copying would be more profitable for the seller of tapes and CDs. Of course, many other possibilities can be imagined, but the conclusion that allowing unfettered copying might improve the revenue position of the copyright owner is clearly feasible.

Note that indirect appropriability implies that the purchasers of CDs in the previous example actually pay copyright owners, albeit indirectly. Fair use, a defense against charges of copyright infringement that in essence allows copying in certain cases (discussed in more detail below), might protect the copiers from legal liability, but it does not prevent the "fair-users" from indirectly paying the copyright owners.

There is at least one documented instance where the impacts of indirect appropriability are strong and where unauthorized copying appears to have benefited copyright owners—that is the case of photocopying discussed below.

Of course, just because indirect appropriability *might* be capable of securing profits doesn't mean that it will succeed in any particular case. An important factor that influences the likelihood that indirect appropriability might work is the variability in the number of copies made of each original. Note that in the CD-automobile-cassette example, each CD was used to make one tape; therefore, no variability existed in the number of copies per original. If each CD had been used to make two cassette copies, that would not have changed the story since there still would not have been variability. But if some CDs were used to make no copies, and others were used to make 1,000 copies, then indirect appropriability becomes difficult or impossible.

In the photocopying case to be discussed in detail below, the number of copies made from originals is quite different for two types of originals since library users make many photocopies from each original whereas personal subscribers make few copies. Because the seller is able to distinguish between the two groups and charge the two groups different prices, indirect appropriability can work. But the greater the variability in the number of copies made from each original, the more difficult the task of identifying how many copies are made from each original and charging appropriate prices for originals based on that number of copies. In many cases it will be impossible to charge different prices to different users for identical originals, since sellers will usually not be able to identify the purchaser's copying intent when the original is purchased.

Therefore, in an atmosphere of rampant copying and considerable variability in the number of copies made from each original, the seller will generally find it impossible to identify which originals should have the higher price and successfully charge that higher price. That is why instances of illicit organized copying where a single original might be used by a copier to make thousands of copies are so much more dangerous to copyright holders than unorganized copying where individuals make one or two copies for themselves.

Note also that, when copying occurs, the least variation in the number of copies made from originals tends to occur *when copying is ubiquitous and similar*. Therefore, if some copying is difficult to stop, it might be profitable for copyright owners to encourage everyone to engage in the same degree of copying because that can afford the copyright holder some degree of appropriability. This has interesting implications for Napster and other digital distribution techniques as discussed below.

There is one other form of indirect appropriation worth noting. In some instances, legislation may allow copyright owners to collect revenue in a manner other than charging for use. For example, a tax could be imposed on blank audiotapes or recorders.[16] But this would not directly charge users for the right to copy, since audiotapes can be used to tape works for which copyright clearance was given or for taping non-copyrighted works. For example, people buying digital audiotapes pay an additional amount that goes to the copyright owners but is only indirectly related to actual copying of copyrighted works. We can refer to this as *explicit* indirect appropriability as opposed to the *implicit* indirect appropriability described earlier. On the other hand, an organization such as the Copyright Clearance Center (CCC) tries to directly appropriate revenues for the copyright owners. The CCC gathers rights from publishers and provides licenses to libraries to make copies upon payment to the CCC—with the payment being a function of how much and what is copied based on CCC surveys of copying activity in the libraries.

The Economic Impacts of Previous New Technologies on Copyright Owners

Each new copying technology might appear to require fresh analysis as each generation argues that the new technologies created during its watch require total upheavals of the status quo, whether it is the advent of sound recordings, television, photocopiers, or, in the most recent instance, the Internet. But history tells us that when it comes to copyright, the more things change, the more they remain the same. I believe that copyright law has generally been successful in balancing the costs and benefits to both users and producers as technologies have changed. The trick, or course, is in getting it right. Some of the major technological challenges are listed below.

Photocopying

The ability to photocopy books and magazines with ease might have been thought to jeopardize the livelihood of authors and publishers. After all, anyone could take a copyrighted work and make copies on the photocopier without paying the copyright owner. Yet the photocopier proved a boon to those whose works were most frequently copied.[17]

This occurred for two reasons. First, publishers were able to appropriate a portion of this additional value thanks to indirect appropriability. Second, the convenience of being able to make copies was so great that the nature of scholarship changed among the academic communities that used much of the copyrighted materials that were copied, and the market for journals grew relative to the market for books.

The mechanism underlying this growth in journals was indirect appropriability.[18] Publishers were able to identify those locations where photocopying of copyright materials occurred most frequently—libraries and other similar institutions—and which materials were most frequently photocopied—academic journals. Publishers then began charging a much higher price for library subscriptions relative to personal subscriptions, often two, three, or four times as much. The price differentials between institutional and personal subscriptions to academic journals that are now practically ubiquitous did not exist before the photocopier arrived on the scene.

Further, prior to the advent of the photocopier, researchers needed to either have a personal subscription to a journal or take notes in a library. Books tended to be on single topics, as opposed to journals, which contained articles on varying topics and would therefore have different levels of attraction to different scholars. Books were a key form of scholarship and were deemed of great use. Photocopying changed this relationship. The inconvenience and cost of photocopying entire books was prohibitively high so that they were rarely copied. Articles in journals, on the other hand, were well suited to the photocopier and became the major target of copying activities. Photocopying articles was fast and cheap. Subscriptions were no longer necessary except for those individuals who valued a large percentage of the articles in a journal. Having a photocopy of an article was such an improvement, in terms of convenience and accuracy, over handwritten notes taken in the library that articles and journals became a far more important means of transmitting information than had previously been the case. Books, on the other hand, diminished significantly in importance, as measured by share of library expenditures.[19]

The price discrimination that the advent of the photocopier engendered may or may not have increased overall appropriability. The evidence does not allow sufficient precision to determine the answer to this question. Clearly, however, photocopying did not harm copyright owners of photocopied materials, as made clear by the extremely rapid growth in the number of academic journals relative to the population of readers and also by the financial health of the publishers. The claims by journal publishers to the contrary, and there were many such claims, were an example of crying wolf.

Videocassette Recording: The Betamax Case

The Betamax case played a central role in the Napster defense.[20] The 1984 Supreme Court ruling allowed individuals to legally make private recordings of television shows on their videocassette recorders (VCRs). The Betamax case (so called because at the time the case was brought, VHS had not yet begun its obliteration of the Beta video format) represented another instance where copying was unlikely to harm copyright owners.[21]

Almost all television viewing in the early 1980s was of advertising-supported over-the-air broadcasts, particularly those of the big three networks—ABC, CBS, and NBC. The original Betamax had only a one-hour recording time. The major use for VCRs was expected to be the "time-shifting" of programs for more convenient viewing. Although VCR controls made it possible for viewers to fast-forward through commercials, close attention had to be paid to avoid fast-forwarding through the programming.[22] Thus, time-shifting was unlikely to significantly lower the revenues that would be derived by television broadcasters.[23] The Court concluded that time-shifting was unlikely to harm copyright owners.

Although the Court did not rely on this argument, it was also fairly clear that the amount of time-shifting would be small. For one thing, a single VCR could either make a recording or play one back, but it could not do both simultaneously. Combine this with the fact that the average household viewed six or seven hours of TV a day, including virtually uninterrupted viewing during prime-time programming, and a constraint on behavior very quickly takes hold. If a family were going to watch three hours of prime-time television on Monday, they could not also watch a tape. If they watched a tape of the previous night's programming, they could not record the programming that was on while they watched the tape (unless they had a second VCR, which was quite rare at that time). Therefore, when it came to taping broadcast television for later viewing, it was apparent that not much of this activity was going to occur.

Of course, we know in hindsight that VCRs are used primarily to play prerecorded tapes. Ridiculing the difficulty of setting up VCRs to tape programs unattended has become a staple of second-rate comedians, and time-shifting has not played the damaging role that copyright owners expected it to play. Nor is there much evidence that individuals have been excessively copying prerecorded videotapes, although it is the case that many prerecorded tapes do have a fairly primitive antibackup technology built in.

The difficulty of avoiding commercials, combined with the fact that the amount of time-shifting had to be small, made it apparent that videorecording was not going to harm copyright owners substantially. Fortunately, the Supreme Court managed to get it right, albeit by a narrow 5–4 vote. Several years later, Hollywood learned that by lowering the price of popular prerecorded movies from one hundred dollars to twenty dollars, they could sell far more of them. Today, the revenue from videotaped movies generates more revenue than do theatrical performances.[24] Hollywood's claim of impending doom was just one more in a string of instances of copyright holders crying wolf.

Audiotaping

Even without a high-profile case such as Betamax, audiotaping was a significant issue in the early 1980s, as illustrated by the quote from Alan Greenspan at the beginning of this chapter. The basic mechanism of how indirect appropriability might work with respect to audiotapes was illustrated above. Note that if unauthorized copying were prohibited, copyright holders might actually be worse off. In a world with no copying, record producers might find that consumers would be unwilling to pay as much for CDs, lowering revenues and profits. (It is not clear how many, if any, of the former copiers would purchase legal copies.)[25]

As noted, controlling the variability in the number of copies made from each original was crucial for allowing indirect appropriability to work. It is most likely the case that instances of home audiotaping were common and similar enough to one another that no great harm was likely to be done to copyright owners. Despite dire predictions, the recording industry went on its merry way, merely substituting CDs for vinyl recordings as time progressed.[26] Inaction on the part of Congress and the presumption that most of the copying that was going on was unstoppable and a legitimate exercise of fair use was almost certainly the correct decision.

In response to the dire warnings from the recording industry, Congress considered legislation, but it wasn't until a decade later that the Audio Home Recording Act of 1992 was passed, and it was largely concerned with digital tape recording. That act, which was considered a compromise between creators and users, allows personal copying but requires that recording devices include systems to prevent "serial copying," i.e., making second-generation copies, or copies of a copy. Additionally, the law has provisions to require producers of these recording devices and recording media to pay a tariff for each unit produced or imported. The original target of this law, digital audiotapes (DAT), never achieved any serious market penetration. The devices that have achieved much greater penetration, CD-writers on computers, are not considered recording devices and do not have these copy-protection features; nor have the producers been paying duties. Since the anticopying technology built into DAT players didn't envision the advent of MP3 files (which are very compressed versions of the digital file format found on CDs), the entire MP3 phenomenon would have bypassed these controls on copying anyway.

Digitized Networked Copying: Lessons from the Napster Case

As we have seen, the entertainment industry has often exaggerated the damage to itself that each new copying technology—from cassette tapes and videorecorders to MP3s and Napster—would bring. Crying wolf too many times, however, shouldn't by itself negate claims that a new technology will harm copyright owners. Napster and its descendants (as well as movie and electronic book-copying technologies) appear to be instances where real harm is a possibility.

The Napster program, created by then-teenager Shawn Fanning, provided users with the ability to search for songs encoded in near-CD-quality MP3 format and to identify other computer owners willing and able to transfer those songs. Programs that allow one computer user to interact and exchange files located on other computers that are not full-time servers create a type of network that is known as peer-to-peer. Napster was a peer-to-peer-based program, albeit with a central server to allow users to find one another. Napster grew at an explosive pace and soon had millions of users.[27] As Napster grew in popularity, so did potential investors, interested in the brand name and the millions of eyeballs reached by the Napster program and its Web site.

Some Napster supporters claim that the online sharing of songs is a latter-day Betamax scenario. They argue that Napster users actually purchase more CDs because Napster allows listeners to sample music with which they might otherwise be unfamiliar. But given the fact that files downloaded from Napster are, or at least soon will be, very good substitutes for the original, and since they can be burned onto CDs and copied to increasingly popular MP3 players, it seems likely that these files will substitute for the actual purchase of authorized CDs. Until recently, most downloaders of MP3 files were not able to transfer them onto CDs to be used on the primary stereo system. Empirical testing at this early stage in the development of the MP3 market is therefore likely to find much smaller negative impacts than are likely to occur later. Further, although some sampling undoubtedly occurs, the direction of its impact is unclear, as shown below, and it seems intuitively unlikely that sampling could reverse the negative impacts on copyright holders that would be expected from the substitution of computer files for purchased CDs.

Unlike the audiocassette example mentioned above, Napster-style copying is unlikely to allow record companies to indirectly capture the value of the copies being made from legal originals since some originals will have dozens or hundreds of copies made and others none. Nor does it seem likely that the amount of copying will be small—there are no time constraints or confusing instructions to prevent widespread copying. Finally, copies are likely to serve as substitutes for the purchase of originals in this case. The people making the copies are the very group that was expected to purchase originals. (That is why it is not surprising that surveys indicate that Napster users are among the heaviest purchasers of CDs.)

The Impact of Peer-to-Peer Networks on Revenues—The Theory

Napster (now largely dismantled by court order) appeared to be a clear threat to the revenues of copyright owners of recorded music. The number of individuals using Napster at its peak had reached approximately 70 million.[28] Many of these users were concentrated in the groups of users most responsible for the purchase of recorded music—teenagers and young adults. The record companies' fear of Napster was not irrational: The market is to some extent political, and if enough users decided that they wanted to trade music files for free, they could get Congress to legislate their desires into law. That helps to explain the urgency demonstrated by the courts and the copyright owners.

But it is not obvious that file-sharing over the Internet hurts the revenues of copyright owners, nor even that it decreases appropriability. As discussed above, copying need not have the detrimental impact that is so often wrongly attributed to it. As is almost always the case, however, theory by itself cannot really tell us what impact peer-to-peer networks such as Napster would have on copyright owners. But it certainly can provide a good deal of guidance about the likely outcome.

There are two possible means by which Napster-style copying

may nonetheless not harm revenues of copyright holders—indirect appropriability and exposure effects.

Indirect Appropriability

First we have the possibility of indirect appropriability. Recall how peer-to-peer networks function—files on individuals' computers become part of the database sharable among all those logged on to it. One can construct a scenario whereby each individual buys half the quantity of CDs that they would normally buy and downloads the other half from the network (assuming individuals continue to listen to the same number of songs). This may not be a totally unrealistic assumption since many individuals would need to have duplicate CDs, or at least duplicate files; otherwise, everyone trying to download a song from a single original CD stored on one machine would run up against limited bandwidth from that individual's machine. Even though the number of copies grows exponentially, since copies can be made of copies, it is still more problematic and time-consuming to start from a very small than from a very large number of originals. With very few sales of original CDs, it would be more difficult for a very large number of users to successfully download the song during the period of its peak popularity.[29]

At any rate, one could imagine record companies selling half the number of CDs that they would have sold in the absence of copying. The question is whether the companies could then charge approximately twice the price (setting aside for argument's sake that part of the rationale given for downloading is the high cost of today's CDs), allowing them to appropriate roughly the same value as before. This could occur if Napster enforced a rule stating that the number of files downloaded had to match the number of files uploaded. In such a case, having a file that is in heavy demand would be valuable for those wishing to generate credits with which to later download files. Under such a regime, we would expect users to be willing to pay a higher price to purchase the original CDs early in the process when it would be difficult to get a downloaded copy to make available to others. Further, if it were possible to change the code in recordings (as the 1992 Home Recording Act envisioned) so that copies could only be made from an original, not from a copy of an original, then users of the system would be required to purchase CDs if they wanted to download songs. If the system were "balanced" sufficiently, one can imagine indirect appropriability working to keep both revenues and appropriability intact.

But, of course, Napster in its original format had no such rule requiring uploads before downloads could proceed. Users did not have to earn credits in order to download files. Under the actual procedures followed by Napster, which did not require any quid for the quo, Napster users who purchased legitimate copies had no incentive to pay a higher price to allow unnamed and unknown users to download their files on Napster.

Finally, some (for example, Stanford law professor Lawrence Lessig, the author of *Code and Other Laws of Cyberspace*) have argued that an explicit indirect means of appropriability could be put in place, as discussed earlier in the case of taxing digital audio tapes.[30] Lessig used the example of cable retransmission of broadcast signals although similar analogies could be made to cable networks' use of music. In each of these cases, cable operators pay for the right to transmit programs or music, but the price is set by a governmental body, not by the copyright owner. Lessig argues that this is preferable to a negotiated price. These analogies, however, are inappropriate.

In the instances mentioned by Lessig, such as cable retransmission, the users of the copyrighted material (i.e., cable networks) pay some portion of their revenues to copyright owners in the form of performance or retransmission rights.[31] Such indirect payments work because these uses are *additional* or *incremental* uses and do not remove the revenues that copyright owners received in their original markets. Thus, this new source of revenue would be a net gain to the copyright owner, an instance of making the pie bigger but also increasing the absolute size of the piece going to the copyright owner whether or not the share of the pie goes up. One can argue about whether the payments are too high or too low, but these extra uses cannot leave the copyright owner worse off than before.

In the case of Napster and other peer-to-peer systems, however, this logic doesn't work. Using music from peer-to-peer systems is likely in many cases to substitute for the purchase of a CD.[32] For this reason, it is not just a case of Napster creating additional value without payment but one of Napster reducing payments in the original markets. Napster is not a new use of copyrighted music with the only problem being one of allocating revenues. Napster provides the means to destroy the old market. If Napster had been allowed to continue in its original guise, it is unlikely that the revenues it generated, for example, from advertising, would have been as large as the losses it imposed in the CD market, and thus even a tax of 100 percent would not have made copyright owners whole, to say nothing of giving them a piece of a new market.[33] Napster may very well have made the pie smaller. So Lessig's suggestion is not a useful antidote for the damage done to copyright owners by the rampant copying engendered by Napster.

Alternatively, a tax could be imposed on the activity of making copies. Using digitized music on one's computer requires the computer, a hard drive, a sound card, and, possibly, rewriteable CDs and drives. Unlike the use of audiocassettes, however, the vast majority of computer use is not for the purpose of duplicating copyrighted material; therefore it doesn't make sense to tax computers, hard drives, or sound cards. That leaves the rewriteable CD and blank recordable CDs. If these drives are used primarily for recording copyrighted material, they should already have to pay a small tariff under current law.[34] It is possible that these devices have sufficient noninfringing uses that they are properly classified as noninfringing. So there might not even be an appropriate target on which to place a tax.

Exposure Effects

Then, of course, there is the possibility that peer-to-peer systems might help copyright owners by making it easier for users to sample songs. If Napster were merely used to "try out" a song or an album, as might be done in a record store or by listening to the radio, then Napster use would be a complement to a CD purchase, not a substitute for one. In fact, Napster's experts in its court hearings have made this claim, the evidence for which will be examined in more detail in the next section. Of course, the difference between listening to a song in a store or on the radio and listening to the song using Napster is that, in the latter case, an actual physical representation of the song is in the possession of the user whereas, in the former cases, only the memory of the tune remains in the user's possession.

Even if Napster were used merely for sampling, its impact on the CD market need not be the benevolent one espoused by Napster's supporters. The usual assumption is that, if Napster merely helps people decide which CDs to purchase, it cannot be harmful and would most likely be beneficial to the copyright owner. Since Napster is only providing information to consumers—or so the argument goes—this activity must benefit society as well as copyright owners. From this perspective, thanks to Napster, consumers are better able to select songs that provide the greatest enjoyment for the time and money expended. It seems natural that they should then be willing to pay more for the CDs they purchase.

As appealing as this story is, however, it is not correct and can be quite misleading.[35] The fact that the consumer is better able to satiate his desire for music with the CDs that he purchases implies that the number of CDs actually purchased would quite possibly fall.

With better sampling, CDs purchased provide greater utility because they better fit the desires of consumers; therefore consumers have a higher willingness to pay.[36] But assuming that CDs all basically meet the same need for music consumption, the CDs purchased provide greater value and do a better job of satiating the desires of the consumers. So consumers may discover that they do not need to purchase as many CDs, since their thirst for music can be quenched with fewer of them.[37] Depending on supply conditions, it can be shown that the total quality of CDs, their price, and the total revenue in the market may go either up or down.[38]

This can be fairly easily demonstrated using the economist's favorite tool, supply and demand. In essence, the ability of consumers to better select CDs will rotate the market demand curve for CDs clockwise, from D1 to D2 in figure 7-1. The demand curve rotates in this manner because the initial CDs purchased now provide greater utility since they better fit the desires of consumers; therefore consumers have a higher willingness to pay. But, assuming that all CDs basically meet the same need for music consumption, there is less value placed upon the purchase of later CDs since the need for music is met so well by the early CDs pur-

Figure 7.1.

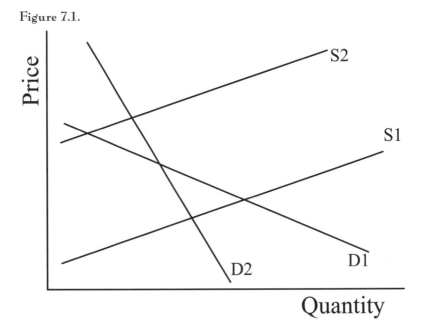

chased. Depending on the position of the supply curve, the total quantity of CDs, their price, and the total revenue in the market may go either up or down.

With a supply curve such as S2, both the price and quantity of CDs purchased go up when better sampling shifts demand from D1 to D2, so that Napster would increase revenues and quantity in this instance. However, with a supply curve such as S1, lying below the intersection of the two demand curves, the quantity, price, and revenues will fall when better sampling causes demand to shift from D1 to D2. Note, of course, that the area under D2 must be greater than the area under D1 at the two intersections because greater information leads to greater efficiency.[39] Thus, with S1, the quantity of CDs, the revenue generated, and the degree of appropriability all fall when sampling is enhanced.

The Impact of Napster on Revenues—The Evidence

In the Napster case (*A&M Records v. Napster*) a group of record companies brought suit in the Northern District of California against Napster, the leading online server-based peer-to-peer system. The hearing took place in the fall of 2000, and a preliminary injunction barring Napster from allowing users to download copyrighted files was granted in March 2001. The evidence put forward in the hearings on the preliminary injunction against Napster consisted of a set of expert reports by economists, marketers, and others that were mainly focused on two issues:[40] first, whether or not Napster was likely to increase or decrease sales of CDs in the market and second, whether or not Napster's existence as then configured would handicap the nascent market for the legitimate selling of music online. Unfortunately, the evidence from these reports provides very little in the way of useful guidance on these issues. Nevertheless, a great deal of misinformation has been put forward about these reports, so I will comment on them at some length.

These expert reports were conducted for the purposes of the hearing on the preliminary injunction to stop Napster from trans-

mitting copyrighted materials and not for a complete trial.[41] Therefore, it is to be expected that the reports might not have the level
of sophistication and completeness that might come about in a full
case. Nevertheless, the hearing on the injunction had very high
visibility, and several of the experts were quite well known. Additionally, most of these reports (or their authors) were challenged
according to court rules on the qualifications of experts. The lower
court's rulings on these challenges were illuminating for the hostility they showed toward the Napster experts, a hostility that I
believe indicated a predisposition of the judge against Napster.
Additional evidence on Judge Patel's impartiality, or lack of it,
came in her nonsensical and later overruled "zero-tolerance" ruling threatening to shut down Napster for any trivial illegal copying
that it was unable to prevent.[42]

A majority of the reports focused on whether or not Napster
was decreasing the sale of CDs. As already explained, one might
expect Napster's impact to be quite small due to the difficulty of
using Napster downloads on the home stereo. In an attempt to
demonstrate harm, the plaintiffs had as their centerpiece two reports—one that examined the pattern of CD sales in stores near
college campuses (the Fine Report) and the other a survey of college students asking them about their views on Napster and its
impact on some of their musical habits (the Jay Report).[43] The
defense had its own survey of Napster users (the Fader report)
and several critiques of the Fine report.

In principle, a statistical analysis of how actual CD sales were
impacted by the popularity of Napster is far preferable to a methodology based on surveys. For one thing, surveys are self-reported,
and most Napster users were probably aware that Napster was in
legal difficulty. For this reason, survey respondents might find it
in their self-interest to minimize any evidence that Napster actually decreased their purchases of CDs. It is somewhat (though
much less dramatic) like asking death-row convicts whether the
death penalty is a deterrent to murder. Further, even if respondents were to tell the truth, it is unclear if they would actually

know what impact Napster had had on their behavior. Respondents might very well not know with any precision how much they spend on CDs per month. Unless they track their expenses very carefully, their impressions of the impact of Napster on their behavior may very well be incorrect. They might in fact buy some CDs because of the songs they downloaded from Napster, and this might color their impressions even if they purchase fewer CDs overall.

Statistical analysis of actual sales is really the only way to determine what Napster's impact was. Unfortunately, the statistical analysis of CD sales reported in the Fine report provides ambiguous answers. The Fine report examines sales at CD retailers near college campuses and compares the sales trends in those stores to those of other CD retailers.[44] The theory is that students at college campuses use the Internet and Napster more than do typical consumers. Therefore, any differences in the behavior of sales between the two groups of stores should be due to Napster. Although Fader, one of the Napster experts, criticizes the focus on college students, this focus is a very practical, if imperfect, way of isolating the overall impact of Napster. Despite claims to the contrary, it seems unlikely that the behavior of Napster users who are not college students is so different as to counteract the measured impact on college students, especially since many of the other users are high-school students.

This particular study design, although potentially useful, has some serious problems with its implementation. One major problem with the Fine study, as both Fader and Hall point out at length, is that it neglects to control for the impact that online purchases of CDs, as opposed to downloads of songs, might have had on bricks-and-mortar record stores near college campuses. Internet merchants such as Amazon and CDNOW increased their CD sales during the period of Napster's growth. Since Internet access is a requirement for both using Napster and ordering online, it is possible that college students have merely switched their patronage from bricks-and-mortar retail outlets to online retailers.[45]

Napster experts Hall and Fader claim that the Fine Report is fatally flawed by this oversight. In principle, however, it could be corrected if data were available for online retailers and the two groups of bricks-and-mortar retailers on, for example, a monthly basis, along with data on the number of songs being downloaded on Napster.[46] Instead, however, the Fine study presents data that are very coarse: once-a-year data from the first quarter of 1997 to the first quarter of 2000. Given Napster's brief existence (it became publicly available in August of 1999), the data that are supposed to reveal Napster's influence amount to but a single before-and-after snapshot of the impact of Napster.

What does the Fine study find? Mr. Fine focuses on the fact that, from the first quarter of 1999 to the first quarter of 2000 (Napster came into existence at about the midpoint of this period), sales at bricks-and-mortar CD stores near colleges fell by 2 to 3 percent but rose at other bricks-and-mortar CD stores by approximately 7 percent. From this, Fine concludes that Napster led to a decrease in sales of CDs at stores near colleges. Fine's conclusions are undermined, however, by his data for earlier years. From 1998 to 1999, a year preceding Napster's existence, sales near colleges fell by about 5 percent while rising elsewhere by approximately 3 percent. If bricks-and-mortar CD retailers near colleges were not performing as well as other bricks-and-mortar CD retailers prior to Napster's introduction, the fact that they continued to do relatively poorly after Napster's introduction can hardly be taken as evidence that Napster is responsible for the difference.

The data, in fact, are more consistent with the theory that online sales are replacing bricks-and-mortar sales than with the claim that Napster is hurting sales.[47] The fact that Napster could, at most, have influenced these figures for about six months, a period during which it would have had the smallest number of users, makes these data less useful than data based on later time periods. It is unfortunate that Mr. Fine chose only four time periods to examine, but it is fortunate, although not for his client, that he provides more than two years' worth of data.

Napster's experts preferred to focus on the continued robust growth of CD sales overall, after even after Napster's birth. Certainly, this growth, the 7 percent figure at bricks-and-mortar stores reported above, is inconsistent with the idea of "irreparable" harm claimed in the preliminary injunction, particularly considering that Napster downloads were reported to be four times as large as the number of legitimately purchased songs. But it hardly demonstrates that Napster had a benign impact on CD sales since there might well have been other factors at work, and the increase in CD sales might have been even larger without Napster's impact.

A major impediment to measuring Napster's long-term impact during this period is that MP3 files, the format used on Napster, were not initially very good substitutes for CDs (although they have since become better substitutes and continue to improve). At first, MP3 files could generally be listened to only on computers and could not be played on the home audio system (unless the computer was hooked up to the home system). That may help explain why Napster's impact on sales was not apparent at the time the analysis was performed. As MP3 use has increased, however, more and more audio components have been converted to play MP3 files. Also, most users were downloading files over slow telephone modems so the impact was probably not as large as it would have been had higher bandwidth connections been more readily available.[48] As more computer users adopt CD-writing hardware, MP3 files are being converted back into CD formats that are playable through normal audio systems. Over time, it is likely that MP3 files would have become better substitutes for CDs and would have been played more frequently on primary audio systems. If this had happened, the predicted negative impact of Napster would have been more likely to be noted—if it had not been shut down.

The other category of report presented in the Napster case is based on surveys. As noted, the results from surveys should be regarded with great skepticism. The Recording Industry Association of America presented a survey of college students by Deborah

Jay, a marketing consultant who attempted to infer whether Napster increased or decreased the purchase of CDs based on answers given to questions that do not directly address the point. Jay concluded that 41 percent of Napster's subscribers used it in ways that displaced the purchase of CDs. But the fact that Jay did not ask this question directly of her subjects makes her conclusions suspect. Further, her categorization of answers as enhancing or decreasing CD sales is questionable and seems to favor a negative finding about Napster's impacts. On the other hand, the bias from respondents trying to support Napster might work in the other direction.

As an example of these problems, consider her classification of responses to an open-ended question asking respondents why they use Napster. Two of the categories of answers—"buy fewer CDs" and "make my own CDs"—are classified as indicating a substitution of Napster files for CD sales. The first answer obviously fits this characterization. The second, however, is not at all clear. If someone wished to sample music for later purchase and created a CD to sample the music on a stereo system, Jay would classify that answer as indicating that the respondent uses Napster to decrease CD purchases. The fact that Jay doesn't provide separate numbers for each of these two answers makes it impossible to determine whether this is a potentially serious problem or not. Further complicating this issue is the fact that 22 percent of respondents say they either buy fewer CDs or make their own CDs, whereas 8.4 percent say they purchase more CDs.[49] This classification seems capricious. Why not just tell us how many say they purchase fewer CDs instead of lumping them in with those who make their own CDs?

Peter Fader, a marketing professor from the Wharton School who was hired as an expert by Napster, criticized Jay for using only college students, and also for her interpretation of open-ended questions. Although I do not believe his criticism on the use of college students is valid, the concern with Jay's interpretation of open-ended questions seems quite legitimate.

Fader conducted his own survey for Napster that tried to answer the same question. He concludes that Napster decreases CD sales for 8.1 percent of the respondents but increases sales for 28.3 percent of the respondents, virtually the opposite of the conclusion reached by Jay. Fader, however, was harshly criticized by Judge Patel, who questioned both his credentials and the degree to which he participated in the conduct of the study bearing his name.[50] It appears that he did not supervise the execution of the study as closely as he might have. Nevertheless, the harshness of the court's criticism of Fader contrasts with its generally benign view of the problems in the Jay report.

There were other reports, particularly those by economists David Teece, on behalf of the record companies, and Robert Hall, on behalf of Napster. Teece's report is unavailable due to its frequent use of confidential information. He appears to have examined the impact of Napster on the current CD market as well as nascent or planned online sales of music by copyright owners. He concluded that damage to copyright owners is clear. Hall, on the other hand, concluded that Napster increased CD sales because, in his view, it largely allowed users to sample music before purchase.[51] Once again, the court was much harsher in its discussion of Napster expert Hall than in its discussion of Teece.[52] Without seeing Teece's report, however, it is hard to gauge the validity of the court's relative rankings.[53]

All in all, my reading of the reports in the case indicates that the plaintiffs failed to make as persuasive a case for harm as the defense did for the lack of harm.[54] Nevertheless, I believe Napster was probably dangerous to the industry. The inability of the experts to demonstrate harm may be due to the fact that the MP3 files were not yet good substitutes for CDs—most ordinary stereo systems cannot play MP3 files, and CD writers are not yet prevalent enough to allow most users to convert MP3s to audio CDs; even with the equipment the conversion takes some effort. Although the courtroom decision was technically a victory for the record industry, it isn't clear to me that the record industry's strategy was a wise one.

Pure Peer-to-Peer Technologies: The Devil You Don't Know

Napster is not the only game in town. A new generation of programs plays by a somewhat different set of rules. These are programs based on the Gnutella protocols or some variation, programs such as BearShare, Aimster, Limewire, Morpheus (FastTrack), and others. The important difference between these programs and Napster is that these systems are more decentralized—there are often no central servers keeping track of the downloads and uploads.[55]

Obviously, songs downloaded using these programs are likely to have the same type of direct impacts on revenues as does Napster. One question is whether they could be as popular as Napster. If current evidence is to be believed, they are already more heavily used than Napster was at its peak.[56]

This poses an extremely serious problem for copyright enforcement. Because there is no centralized location, firm, individual, or server that can be monitored and controlled by legal authorities, copyright enforcement is going to be very messy at best and impossible at worst. There is a provision in the Digital Millennium Copyright Act (DMCA) that requires Internet Service Providers to block access when notified that users are serving up copyright material using the ISP's facilities. The Motion Picture Association of America (MPAA) has brought action asking ISPs to crack down on users providing movies on pure peer-to-peer-based systems when the MPAA is able to monitor those systems and determine the Internet Protocol (IP) addresses of those allowing movies to be copied.[57] This is not likely to be a successful long-term tactic since it would seem to require static IP addresses. Users have a choice of ISPs, and it would be possible for many users to move to systems that use dynamic IP addresses on high-speed lines such as Earthlink's DSL service. Also, the vast majority of users still use slow dial-up access, and these also have dynamically assigned IP addresses.

It is disturbing to imagine various police authorities monitoring otherwise law-abiding individual computer users and then prosecuting copyright infringers, often teenagers, for downloading music and other files. Yet that is exactly the specter that faces the copyright owners, who do seem willing to undertake it. They might do well to consider, however, the public relations fiasco that ASCAP (American Society of Composers, Authors, and Publishers) created when it decided to enforce copyright against summer camps, including the Girl Scouts, who believed they were no longer allowed to sing copyrighted songs around the campfire.[58] The blizzard of negative publicity engendered by that action required ASCAP to backpedal at full speed. Teenagers trading copyrighted songs may not create the same degree of empathy as young girls singing around the campfire, but lots of parents have such teenagers, and the record industry will have to be very careful not to alienate the public while punishing otherwise law-abiding infringers.

If enforcement against the pure peer-to-peer systems does prove more difficult, how does the possibility of indirectly appropriating revenues stack up? At first blush, one might think that, because there is no central server, these pure peer-to-peer systems are rather like the more traditional exchanges of music or CDs that occur between friends. But that is not the case. These peer-to-peer networks search out other computers running the relevant software and seem capable of finding an enormous number of such computers, far more than any circle of personal friends. On the other hand, there is some indication that users downloading but not uploading files may be ostracized by other copyright violators since several of these programs have "antifreeloading" tools (a delicious irony) to prevent users who are not sharing their own files from being able to download other files.[59]

If "antifreeloading" rules became prevalent, it is possible that the type of balance discussed earlier might arise so that the value of new and popular CDs to users who need to upload songs to "qualify" would increase, and some level of indirect appropriability might be possible. Nevertheless, it seems unlikely that numerous decentralized systems could provide sufficient constraints to reduce "freeloading" and thereby facilitate indirect appropriability on behalf of copyright holders in the way that a centralized system like Napster could (if they so chose).[60] Thus it might have been somewhat shortsighted of the copyright owners to have brought aggressive action against Napster, a relatively easy target, when they might wind up with a much more vibrant decentralized system that will prove far harder to stop or to wrangle indirect revenues from. Napster should have been much easier for copyright holders to deal with. Although the record industry appears to be making peace with Napster, Napster's users have largely gone on to the more decentralized systems. The record industry has won the battle against Napster, but it may find that this action only accelerated its loss of the war against decentralized copying.

Digital Rights Management

The panacea tantalizingly held out to copyright owners, whether the product is music or the written word, is digital rights management (DRM), also known as automated rights management (ARM). DRM refers to technologies that promise to prevent unauthorized copies of copyrighted materials from being made. These mechanisms, buried deep within the digital code of the music or other copyrighted material, also have the ability to allow copies to be made upon payment or to charge "micropayments" for each small use of the product.[61] In principle, such technology could restrict copying—or even just reading—a copyrighted product unless there were a payment.

Of course, forms of copy protection have existed for some time in computer software, videotapes, digital audio tapes, scrambled cable TV signals, and so forth. All have proven susceptible to being cracked by some pirate, somewhere. Even the new technologies are prone to being cracked.[62] Critics of DRM as an encroachment on fair use assign far too much power to this technology. The reason that pirated versions of software, music, and videos have not dominated usage is as much due to the law-abiding nature of users as it is to the difficulty of copying. The fact that digital copies of music are technically better than analog copies is a trivial difference to most listeners not using extremely high-end audio systems.[63]

Copy protection doesn't have to be perfect to do the job. In order to be successful, it merely has to limit the number of pirated copies that are actually used to replace sales. Nevertheless, this modern anticopying technology has aroused concerns that it might abridge our freedoms and tilt the historical balance that exists between users and creators too far in favor of the creator. I now turn to the fulcrum of this balance, which is known as "fair use."

"Fair use" is a legal defense against claims of copyright infringement. There are four factors that are considered in determining whether a use is "fair," and if a use is deemed fair, no copyright payment is required. The four factors are (1) the purpose and character of the use, including whether such use is of a commercial nature or is for nonprofit educational purposes; (2) the nature of the copyrighted work; (3) the amount and substantiality of the portion used in relation to the copyrighted work as a whole; (4) the effect of the use upon the potential market for or value of the copyrighted work. Certain activities such as criticism, comment, news reporting, teaching, scholarship, and research are listed in the copyright statute as exemplars of fair use. There is currently a debate raging about what the impact of DRM will be on fair use and what the consequences will be for society if fair use is largely eliminated.

For scholars and policy analysts, this newest change in technology has led to an outpouring of commentary and analysis with two very distinct schools of thought emerging. On the one hand, the Digital Millennium Copyright Act was created, promoted in large part by sympathetic academics, in response to these perceived dangers to copyright owners who were hoping to forestall or prevent the demise of artistic compensation. On the other hand, scholars such as Pamela Samuelson of Berkeley suggest that these dangers are dramatically overstated and that the attempt to strengthen protection has been overdone.[64] Following in this vein, Lawrence Lessig has suggested that the digitizing of artistic works coded with DRM systems will lead to a far higher level of appropriability than has historically been the case and that technology may have shifted the balance of economic power too far in favor of copyright owners if the government doesn't step in to limit it.[65] Tom Bell of Chapman University, on the other hand, has argued that systems based on DRM, what he calls "fared-use," are logically and legally sound.[66]

In order for DRM to achieve the type of power its critics are so concerned with, "cracking" would need to be close to zero, and analog versions of the material would need to be poor substitutes for the original. The latter requirement does not appear to be met in the real world, making many of the claims of the anti-DRM camp seem unreasonable. Even if DRM made it impossible to cut and paste electronically from one document to the next, one could always just type in the material that one wished to copy into another document.

History tells us that the zero-cracking requirement cannot be achieved through technical sophistication alone. Instead, the powers of the state have to be brought into play, and the DMCA does just that. The DMCA has some draconian provisions to prevent copying, in particular a provision that makes it illegal not just to make copies, but to circumvent, or to create tools that allow the circumvention of, copyright-protection technologies. To violate these provisions of the DMCA, it is not even necessary to make copies of the copyrighted materials. These aspects of the DMCA have raised free speech and civil liberties concerns that go beyond the scope of my expertise, although I am personally troubled by them.

Can DRM shift the balance too far toward copyright owners?

Since Lessig couches his argument against DRM in terms of economics, it is fair to analyze this claim in economic terms.[67] The concern that DRM will somehow cause inefficiency—defined as a reduction in intellectual property produced and used (the "surplus")—is based on two largely false premises.

DRM Will Not Harm "Fair" Use or Any Use

First, the specter of DRM that seems to haunt its critics most is the version in which DRM allows micropayments for each and every use, no matter how small. This would appear to eliminate fair use in its traditional role as a mechanism for allowing copying in those instances where the transaction costs of collecting payment are greater than the payment itself, a view of fair use most often associated with Wendy Gordon,[68] a law professor at Boston University. She has argued that fair use provides a mechanism whereby copying may occur when the transaction costs of getting permission might have been too great to allow even worthwhile copying to occur, an argument similar to that viewing fair use as a form of cost/benefit analysis, which I put forward in my 1981 study. The critics of DRM correctly note that, in general, strengthening copyright and the concomitant reduction in consumption of the copyrighted good (since consumption of unauthorized copies is no longer allowed), might decrease the value to consumers by more than the value of any increased production that might be brought about by the stronger copyright. Fair use, they claim, is a mechanism that needs to be retained to keep the balance from tipping too far (i.e., inefficiently) in this direction.

What the critics of DRM fail to notice in this instance is that the type of micropayment DRM that they so fear does not reduce the consumption of copyrighted goods. By charging for each minor instance of use—each paragraph read or each line of music listened to or each page printed—consumers can be charged amounts that are closely related to their use of the copyrighted product. This extreme form of DRM virtually becomes an instance of "perfect price discrimination," as discussed in chapter 5.[69]

There would no longer be "missed opportunities" whereby copying would not occur because the transaction costs of getting permission were too high relative to the value.

This is in contrast to the normal textbook representation of a market that has but a single price charged to all consumers for identical units of a product. Although a textbook monopolist charges a higher price than is found in a competitive market, it is still but a single price. In this monopoly market, a smaller quantity is therefore sold and consumed. It is the decrease in quantity consumed that is the harm engendered by monopoly; this is what economists refer to as the economic inefficiency of monopoly.[70] On the other hand, when a seller is able to charge several different prices—high prices for users willing to pay high prices and low prices for users unwilling to pay high prices (such as airlines having higher ticket prices for business travelers whose trips usually do not include a Saturday night stayover)—it can lead to increasing inefficiency. The more successfully and completely that a seller can match prices to the maximum prices consumers are willing to pay, the closer the total output will be to the ideal (competitive) level.

Unlike simple monopoly, which restricts output from optimal levels, perfect price discriminators do not restrict output at all. Therefore, they are every bit as efficient as a competitive market, a perfectly standard result that can be found in any textbook.

DRM is not perfect price discrimination. DRM does not charge each consumer an amount exactly equal to his maximum willingness to pay. That ideal can never be achieved. Nevertheless, by tying the usage closely to the payment, DRM will move a good way toward perfect price discrimination. Much of the difference in willingness to pay is a function of how much, how frequently, and how often an item is going to be used. In those instances where there is only a small use of the copyrighted material, DRM can charge a very low price and usage (copying) will not be deterred. Consequently, fair use no longer has an important role to play as an implicit form of cost/benefit analysis.

Admittedly, some of the differences in valuation of the copyrighted good are due to income or taste differences, which DRM doesn't address. The aspect of DRM that most concerns its critics, however, is its ability to charge for each small transaction and to keep copies from being made if payments are not forthcoming.

This is, of course, a purely economic argument, and it turns on the concept of efficiency. Perfect price discriminators, while efficient, remove the "surplus" received by consumers. In layman's terms, the seller sucks up all the difference between the value the consumer puts on the product and its cost of production and converts this difference into profits. Critics of DRM might argue that this is "unfair" to users. But such an argument is not one based on economic efficiency and is not the one that is made by the critics of DRM.

The harm that DRM critics envision, the reduction in use, fair or otherwise, of a copyrighted good is not, in fact, an outcome that is to be expected.

DRM Will Not Reduce Production of New Works

DRM critics, after incorrectly asserting that DRM will reduce consumption of copyrighted materials, then argue that there will be no countervailing benefit, which would usually be the additional production of copyrighted materials brought forth by the additional revenues. This notion that additional revenues will not bring forth additional output arises from an influential paper by Landes and Posner that appeared in the *Journal of Legal Studies* in 1989.[71] Prior to the publication of this paper, it had been taken as a given that increasing copyright increased appropriability and thus incentives to produce. Stronger or longer copyright protection led to more payments to creators, which led to the production of more creative works. It seemed clear enough.

But Landes and Posner broaden that basic model by assuming that new works are often derived, at least in part, from old works, so that making it more difficult for the authors of new works to build upon old works might actually reduce the number of new works.

In spite of the originality of this claim, there are several reasons to believe that the traditional expectation—increasing copyright protection increases the body of copyrighted works—still holds in our world. The Landes/Posner article was examining fundamental questions about copyright, such as whether ideas should be copyrighted, and many of their results make the most sense in a legal setting very different from the actual setting. For example, if someone could claim ownership of the phrase "good morning," asking for payment each and every time it was used, one can imagine the costs being large with no concomitant benefits. Similar problems might arise if someone could copyright ideas, such as the idea of two young people falling in love even though their families disliked one another, and try to prevent others from using that idea.

Actual copyright law, however, limits its protection to the "expression" of ideas, and individuals are allowed to create a particular expression even if the underlying idea has already been created and copyrighted by someone else, as long as it was not copied from someone else's work.[72] Thus, the major hindrance that copyright on old works causes for creators of new works is likely to be when the creators of new works wish to copy direct passages from older works. This is only legitimately done with attribution, however, and such writings tend to be in the nature of reviews or academic works. In these cases, there is little reason to believe that an accommodation would not be made between the creator of the original and the creator of a work that uses part of the original. If the derivative work is hostile to the original, an agreement might not be reached. But it is unusual to have more than a paragraph or two directly quoted at one time, and this can be done the old-fashioned analog way (i.e., typing by hand if necessary). Then we are back in the realm of old-fashioned fair use even if it now serves a somewhat different purpose.[73]

Another concern about DRM is that it appears capable of extending protection indefinitely. In reality, all DRM schemes can be broken, just as all copy protection on software could be broken during the last two decades. Traditional copyright enforcement and the desire of users to remain within the law should limit the distribution of these "cracked" items while the term of copyright is still in force. Once the statutory copyright protection period is over, however, everyone can in good conscience distribute cracked items. DRM, therefore, will not lead to permanent copyright protection. This fact—that copyright protection doesn't last forever—might be one reason to oppose the DMCA's provisions that attempt to prevent all circumvention of protection schemes since such provisions might extend protection indefinitely.

It is fair to conclude, therefore, that increased appropriability brought about by DRM will enhance the production of new copyrighted works. If DRM allows a very strong degree of price discrimination, there will be very little loss from the possibility of users being disenfranchised from purchase by the extra appropriability given to copyright owners. DRM, even if it eliminated fair use, would be economically efficient.[74] Of course, one could always argue that DRM will make authors too rich and readers too poor. Or perhaps that it might lead to some form of censorship.[75] But these are not arguments based on economic efficiency—nor do they seem reasonable.

Finally, although DRM, if it works, will be a salutary development, proposed legislation that appears to require DRM (the Security Systems Standards and Certification Act) is misguided.[76] There is no need to have the government certify which security technologies are to be used or to force a decision on market participants regarding the choice of which, if any, of these technologies, should be used. This is just another case of the government meddling in an area where it serves no useful purpose.

Public Goods, DRM, and Other Alternatives

Copyrighted creations (to be called "titles," a shorthand to distinguish them from reproductions of the good), whether embodied in a CD or a stream of bits over the Internet, are public goods, which, as defined above, means they don't get used up when consumed. Efficient consumption of the title requires that any consumer for whom the title (e.g., a collection of songs) has a value that is above the cost of producing its physical embodiment or reproduction (the CD) be allowed to consume it since allowing such consumption deprives no other consumer of possible consumption. Assume for the moment that the cost of making reproductions is zero. Then, if the price of reproductions were made low enough to allow all potential users to purchase reproductions—in other words, zero—there would be no money to pay the creator of the title.

This is the trade-off that is known to exist in the creation and distribution of public goods. Efficient consumption of reproductions requires a price close to the cost of making reproductions, whereas efficient production requires that producers receive sufficient payment to compensate them for the act of creating titles. Traditional market mechanisms are not expected to be able to produce the theoretically ideal quantity of titles. Too few titles are likely to be produced, and too little consumption of any single title is likely to occur in comparison to the theoretical ideal.

Ironically, the sole market mechanism that can theoretically produce the ideal level of public goods is perfect price discrimination. That is because the perfect price discriminator, by definition, charges each consumer exactly the amount that consumer is willing to pay, thus deterring no consumer from consuming. The ideal consumption level for any title is thus a by-product of perfect discrimination. Further, since the perfect discriminator generates revenues equal to the value the product provides to the consumer, all titles with total values greater than the cost of production are likely to be produced, leading to the production of the optimal number of titles.

That is the direction in which DRM promises to take us. DRM promises to make the payment a function of use. Those who listen to a song more frequently are likely to also have the higher values, and this approaches perfect discrimination. So even if critics of DRM were to refocus their argument to one based on the equity or inequity of having producers taking so much and consumers so little, they would be arguing against economic efficiency, which would be a turnabout of 180 degrees.

Although DRM is one solution to copying and may prove central to resolving the issue of unauthorized copying, there are other potential solutions that might incorporate some of DRM's anticopying characteristics although not the payment mechanisms that are normally associated with DRM.

Some copyright markets, for example television and radio broadcasts, use a device known as a "blanket license" to pay for their use of music. A blanket license allows the purchaser of the license to use any amount of the copyrighted material contained in the repertoire covered by the license while paying a single fee that does not depend on the frequency of the use of the repertoire. Historically, the best-known instances of blanket licenses have been sold by performing rights organizations such as ASCAP and BMI.

These blanket licenses are sold to television and radio stations with the price of the license a function of the revenues earned by the broadcaster. Blanket licenses have some very useful economic characteristics. First, since the cost of using another copyrighted item in the repertoire is zero, consumers who purchase the license use the optimal amount of these public goods. From an economic efficiency vantage, this is much better than selling the individual items in the repertoire one at a time (unless the seller is a perfect price discriminator).

It is, of course, possible that some users may not purchase the blanket license, so there may be an inefficiency on the consumption side anyway, although, in the case of television and radio, all stations have purchased such licenses, and the artificial restriction on the number of stations by regulators tends to ensure that the blanket license fee doesn't reduce the number of stations. Also, since a price based on revenues is likely to be related to willingness to pay (i.e., it approaches perfect price discrimination) the system would appear to have excellent efficiency characteristics given that the products are public goods. There is no reason that a record company could not just as easily employ a similar device in selling music to individual consumers by means of what we might call a blanket subscription.

Sellers of music, among them the new Napster, are publicly discussing subscription systems whereby users are charged some sort of monthly fee for access to some amount of music. A few initial forays into the market have been made. A monthly subscription fee could be like a blanket license as long as it allowed unrestricted use of the copyrighted material covered by the license and didn't limit the number of downloads each month.

It doesn't appear that this is the route that is being taken by the record companies, however. News reports indicate that monthly subscription fees are going to apply to only a fixed number of downloads per month.[77] These reports also indicate that record companies envision a pricing structure of at least ten dollars a month for a limited number of downloads. The downloaded songs, according to initial plans, will not be playable on any devices other than PCs and will be limited in terms of how many times they can be played or copied.[78] For higher prices, a small number of songs can be burned onto CDs.

This is quite different from the blanket license and doesn't have the same efficiency consequences. One might argue that it would be foolish for the record companies to allow unlimited access to their repertoire since consumers would seem to have an incentive to download everything they want all at once and then stop paying. This concern, however, ignores the fact that the vast majority of sales are of new music and that it is the new additions to the repertoire that consumers now purchase; these additions would provide continued incentive to subscribe to a monthly service.

The original pricing plans appear somewhat misguided, but perhaps the record industry knows something others do not. On the other hand, it is possible that they will follow the lead of the movie industry, which initially overpriced prerecorded videotapes because they thought that video rental stores were the primary market. Only when it was discovered that many individual movie viewers actually wanted to purchase videotapes did the price come down to levels that made it affordable for individuals. It isn't really a question of *whether* the sellers will get the price right—the question is rather *when* they will get it right.

Further complicating the issue is the fact that Web sales compete with bricks-and-mortar retail outlets. These outlets that sell CDs should pressure record companies to keep online prices at a high enough level that retail store sales are not discouraged. The initial restriction on the number of burns from a single artist is also consistent with an attempt to keep Web sales from cannibalizing CD sales. Large retail chains have significant leverage on the recording industry. To the extent that a large fraction of sales are made through bricks-and-mortar retailers, Web sales may be forced to remain poor substitutes for CD sales. This could happen in spite of the fact that Web sales are inherently more efficient since they do not incur the costs of packaging, shipping, distribution, or physically producing the CD. This may help explain the seeming unreasonableness of the current prices and restrictions.

Finally, the Music Online Competition Act, proposed recently by Congressman Rick Boucher, a Democrat from Virginia, contains a mandatory form of nondiscriminatory licensing between record companies and distributors in the midst of some useful provisions.[79] The concern seems to be the perennially misguided one that having a monopoly on both the wholesale and retail segments of a single market is somehow worse than just having a monopoly on the wholesale side. Economic analysis does not support this concern. It is quite possible that the music industry, for example, will no longer need the services of a separate distribution channel. If there is little competition in the wholesale segment, the retail segment can do little to change that, and it serves no useful purpose for the government to try to tinker with the contractual relationships that are likely to arise. The only antitrust concern with merit is the possibility that joint ventures between the different record labels might allow a degree of collusive behavior with regard to setting prices. Yet, the nondiscriminatory pricing clause of the Music Online Competition Act is of no value if the nondiscriminatory price is a monopoly price.[80]

The government should not try to prevent the withering of the current separate retail segment since its existence, competitive or otherwise, serves no particular competition-enhancing function. If there is no longer a useful economic function to be served by a separate retail segment—and there might no longer be one—consumers would be better off without it.

The Bottom Line

The impact of pirating has often been misunderstood, and copyright owners have frequently claimed harm when little or none was occurring. This was true for many copying technologies. Nevertheless, record companies and copyright owners are right to fear Internet-based copying of digitized products. It is a potentially serious threat to their well-being. Still, the arguments against Napster and its relatives remain basically theoretical. As strong as they appear to be, it is somewhat premature to say we know what will happen one way or another since there is as yet no compelling empirical support. The evidence that has been put forward up to this time doesn't clearly point even to the direction of the impact, let alone the magnitude.

Even if Napster had been as serious a threat to record companies' and copyright holders' revenues as implied by theory, it is not the most formidable threat facing copyright owners. Pure peer-to-peer pirating would seem to be far more dangerous because Napster could have been tamed by changing its rules, but peer-to-peer networks cannot. By crippling Napster, copyright holders may have strengthened a far more fearsome foe, thus diminishing their chances of appropriating revenues from activities that they might not be able to stop.

In the not too distant future, DRM technology should allow copyright owners to reduce large-scale unauthorized copying. These DRM tools should greatly reduce any harm to copyright owners brought about by unauthorized copying. At that point, Web sites and technologies that allow unauthorized copies should be of far less importance as long as the DRM technology proves difficult enough to break.

Many scholars and commentators fear that DRM is dangerous because its practical elimination of fair use would seem to upset the delicate balance between creators and users. These fears are largely unfounded, at least in terms of economic efficiency. Because price discrimination is enhanced, there is every reason to believe that efficiency is enhanced as well. These critics of DRM imagine it providing more power to authors than it will in reality be able to deliver.

Inexpensive copying technologies, which have been with us for at least forty years, have not as yet caused great damage, notwithstanding the claims of the recording and film industries. Although it is possible that the current generation of copying technologies will in fact live up to the dire predictions of doom coming from the copyright owners, there needs to be some powerful evidence to support this claim before we consider the type of legislation that has already been enacted as well as any new proposals that further trample on individual freedom.

The Internet, as has been the case for many other technologies, should prove a boon, not a blight, to record companies and copyright owners once they learn how to use it effectively. It provides a wonderful improvement in distribution. As was true in the videocassette example, however, record companies will need to experiment to find the appropriate pricing levels for their products. It is possible that some start-up with a better business plan will replace the incumbents, but this is largely irrelevant to the balance between creators and users. Internet distribution should largely destroy bricks-and-mortar record stores, and when it does, the old distribution methodology will seem as primitive as horses and buggies seem today. DRM is likely to be a useful tool in this process.

Notes

1. Testimony on the Home Recording Act before the Senate Judiciary's Subcommittee on Patents, Copyrights, and Trademarks, October 25, 1983.

2. The concept of indirect appropriability, to be defined in more detail below, was first propounded in my 1981 monograph for the Canadian Government, "The Impact of Reprography on the Copyright System," Copyright Revision Studies, Bureau Of Corporate Affairs, Ottawa, 1981. The actual term "indirect appropriability" was coined in my 1985 paper "Copying and Indirect Appropriability: Photocopying of Journals," *Journal of Political Economy* (October 1985): 945–957. The 1981 monograph is available at *http://papers.ssrn.com/sol3/ papers.cfm?cfid=565423&cftoken=13632430&abstract_id=250082.*

3. This focus leaves aside the moral rights to that value that are so important under Napoleonic legal systems but is in keeping with the practical purpose of intellectual-property laws in countries such as the United States.

4. One school of thought at the extremity of these debates is populated by those who believe that no copyright is required at all for an efficient, functioning market for artistic and creative goods. The members of this group believe either that being first in the market provides sufficient appropriability so that no additional legal protection is required, or that sufficient incentive to produce these products exists with other forms of remuneration, perhaps of a nonpecuniary nature, so that legal rules restricting the control of these products to their creators is unnecessary. The former school of thought is represented by Arnold Plant "The Economic Aspects of Copyright in Books," *Economica* (May 1934): 167–195, and R. Hurt and R. Schuch-

man, "The Economic Rationale of Copyright," *American Economic Review* (May 1966). The latter school of thought is represented by organizations such as the Free Software Foundation (at *http://www. gnu.org/fsf/fsf.html*).

5. Because intellectual products are a category of "public good," efficiency requires that each intellectual product be produced in sufficient quantity to allow each user willing to pay a price greater than the reproduction cost to receive the good. I discuss public goods in more detail below.

6. In truth, there is virtually no empirical evidence on the extent to which copyright owners require remuneration to create their artistic works. However, the claim that production requires, to at least some extent, remuneration of the producers, is fully consistent with the usual market principles adduced from numerous other instances. Adam Smith's famous statement that production doesn't come from the "benevolence" of butchers, bakers, or candlestick makers but instead derives from their self-interested behavior certainly has a plethora of empirical evidence to support it.

7. See Edmund W. Kitch, "Elementary and Persistent Errors in the Economic Analysis of Intellectual Property," *Vanderbilt Law Review* 53 (November 2000): 1727.

8. There are actually two definitions of public goods in the economics literature. The first defines them as goods with nonrivalrous consumption, as in the text. The other, more prevalent definition, is from Paul Samuelson and has another component in addition to the assumption of nonrivalrous consumption. The additional component is the inability to exclude individuals from consuming the good, as would be the case for national defense or any good without defined property rights. I believe this latter definition to be far les useful since it conflates two independent ideas that need not have anything to do with one another. Any good for which nonexcludability is a property will not be efficiently produced in markets. And nonexcludability

usually has more to do with laws and technology than with the good itself.

9. This might seem to complicate the policy issues, but it actually simplifies them. If a technology decreased appropriability but increased payments to copyright holders, it would both provide greater incentives to create the copyrighted material and also provide greater value to consumers who get to keep the nonappropriated value. Removing this technology would decrease value regarding both the number of titles and the value received for each produced title and could, therefore, not be economically beneficial.

10. For a review of the economic impacts of copying see Richard Watt, *Copyright and Economic Theory: Friends or Foes?* (Cheltanham: Edward Elgar, 2000). This is the most thorough review of this material that I have found. My only quibble is that he attributes most of the modeling that originated in my 1981 monograph (see note 2) to Stanley Besen and Sheila Kirby, "Private Copying, Appropriability, and Optimal Copying Royalties," *Journal of Law and Economics* 32 (1989): 255–280.

11. One neglected point here is the price that is proffered to the pirate that would lead to his decision to forgo the product as opposed to making a legitimate purchase. There is presumably some price above zero at which the pirate would make a purchase when confronted with this choice. The ability to price discriminate is crucial here and is generally important in judging the impact of copying.

12. See my 1981 monograph referenced in note 2 for a discussion of exposure effects.

13. See Lisa N. Takeyama, "The Welfare Implications of Unauthorized Reproduction of Intellectual Property in the Presence of Demand Network Externalities," *Journal of Industrial Economics* 42 (1994): 155–166; K. R. Conner and R. P. Rumelt, "Software Piracy—An Analysis of Protection Strategies," *Management Science* 37, no. 2 (February 1991): 125–139; Oz Shy and Jacques-Francois Thisse, "A

Strategic Approach to Software Protection," *Journal of Economics and Management Strategy* 8 (1999): 163–190.

14. As discussed in Chapter 2. See Stan J. Liebowitz and Stephen E. Margolis "Network Effects and Externalities" entry in *The New Palgrave's Dictionary of Economics and the Law* (Macmillan, 1998), vol. 2, pp. 671–675.

15. Unless, that is, the extra value that the marginal purchaser of originals receives is zero. This would seem unlikely, however.

16. Such payments are quite common and can be found in many countries including Canada and much of Europe. These payments would normally go to an organization or collective representing copyright owners.

17. The claims in this section are documented in Liebowitz (1981).

18. It is also true that the Copyright Clearance Center (CCC) came into existence to allow copiers to make direct payments to copyright holders. But the improvement in the economic well-being of journal publishers occurred quite independently of the CCC since the CCC was not organized until well after the market for journals had experienced enormous growth. See Liebowitz (1981), pp. 64–68.

19. This is documented in Liebowitz 1981 and 1985 as referenced in note 2 above. Book expenditures were more than three times those of periodicals from the 1940s until the 1960s when the ratio began to fall dramatically and fell to about 1:1 in the early 1980s. In 1996, expenditures on serials outpaced those of books and bound periodicals by 8:5. See table 11 in "The Status of Academic Libraries in the United States," U.S Department of Education, Office of Educational Research and Improvement; NCES 2001-301; May 2001.

20. *Universal Studios Inc. v. Sony Corporation of America,* 1984. The original district court ruling was in 1979.

21. This material is based on Stan J. Liebowitz, "The Betamax Case" (unpublished manuscript, 1987), available on the Social Science Research Network (SSRN.com).

22. It was also the case that remote controls at the time were tethered by wires to the VCR, thus making their use not very convenient.

23. Defendants in the Napster and MP3.com cases argued that their products "space-shifted" music from a CD to a computer, a putative analogy to the time-shifting that occurred in the Betamax case. A problem with this analogy is that without indirect appropriability, space-shifting would decrease revenues to copyright owners, a result not analogous to that of time-shifting since the VCR users were still exposed to commercials. A more important defect in this analogy in the case of Napster is the fact that what Napster does is not actually space-shifting. Since Napster users do not download their own files into their computer, but instead download files from others, it is better described as "user-shifting" than space-shifting. User-shifting could, in other circumstances, be considered a euphemism for "theft" except that the theft is from the copyright owner in the form of a lost potential sale, rather than from the user who provides the original to be copied.

24. According to the U.S. Statistical Abstract, table 909, theatrical movie revenues were thirty-two dollars per person per year in 1998 whereas revenues from prerecorded movies were ninety-two dollars.

25. Silva and Ramello argue that unauthorized home taping helped producers largely by allowing low-valuation consumers to become music listeners and that these users later became the high valuation listeners that record producers wanted. Francesco Silva and Giovanni B. Ramello, "Sound Recording Market: the Ambiguous Case of Copyright and Piracy," *Industrial and Corporate Change* 9 (2000): 415–442.

26. The recent paper by Hui et al., attempts to estimate the harm brought about by the pirating of CDs. They report a small negative impact, but they do not attempt to measure the impact of indirect appropriability. See Kai Lung Hui, I. P. L. Png, and Yan Cui "Piracy and the Legitimate Demand for Recorded Music" working paper, March 2001, *http://www.comp.nus.edu.sg/~ipng/*.

27. In February of 2001, 2.8 billion files were downloaded, the peak number in its history. By April, after Napster was ordered to stop allowing copyrighted music to be transferred, the number had fallen to 1.6 billion. See "Napster Downloads Drop 36 Percent," Reuters, May 2, 2001.

28. This estimate was reported in "Napster Could Face Shutdown," Associated Press, April 10, 2001.

29. With enough time, this bandwidth limitation could be overcome, but the nature of the music business is such that a small number of songs are in extremely high demand for a short period of time. As long as tastes gravitate around the same small number of songs at any one time, the argument holds.

30. See Lawrence Lessig "Just Compensation," *The Industry Standard,* April 18, 2001.

31. When music is put onto a record or CD, the creator of the music receives a small payment for each copy; this is known as a mechanical royalty. Similarly, composers receive a percentage of television, radio, cable, or concert revenues as compensation from broadcasters for the use of their music; this is known as a performing rights payment. When broadcast signals are carried on cable, it is often known as a retransmission right.

32. However, as reported below in the section on Napster's impact on revenues, the current evidence is unclear.

33. It was never clear what Napster's business model was when it was merely allowing the free transfer of files, but one possibility was the sale of advertising. The possible advertising revenues were dwarfed by the potential losses that might have been imposed upon record companies.

34. The Audio Home Recording Act of 1992 provides that importers, manufacturers, or distributors of any digital audio recording device or digital audio recording media must file quarterly statements and pay royalties on each recorder or piece of media distributed in the United States. The royalty is two percent of the manufacturer's selling price for recorders and three percent of the manufacturer's selling price for recordable media. See Robert A. Starrett, "Copying Music to CD: The Right, the Wrong, and the Law," EMedia Professional, February 1998, available at *http://www.cdpage.com/Audio_Compact_Disc/ rightwrong.html.*

35. A typical view is espoused in the expert reports put forward by Napster in its defense. One of those reports, by Robert Hall, states on page 2, "The exchanges of music facilitated by Napster stimulate the demand for the plaintiffs' CDs by allowing consumers to sample CDs and develop interest in CDs that they subsequently purchase." The reports from Napster's experts can be found at *http://napster.com/ pressroom/legal.html.* Several, but not all, of the RIAA's reports can be found at *http://riaa.com/napster_legal.cfm.*

36. In essence, the ability of consumers to better select CDs will rotate the market demand curve for CDs clockwise.

37. Another way of looking at this is to imagine that some CDs that are now purchased are "mistakes" due to insufficient information. With the additional information provided by the Napster experience, fewer of these mistakes are made, and fewer CDs are purchased.

38. By analogy, it is as if CDs were chocolate bars (or light bulbs). These bars are bought in order to eat the chocolate. If each bar were to contain more chocolate (or each bulb were to last twice as long), holding the price of a bar constant, the number of bars sold could go up or down depending on the elasticity of demand for the underlying product of interest, chocolate. If the elasticity of demand for chocolate were greater than one, the now lower effective price of chocolate would lead to an increase in total revenue spent on chocolate and, with the price of bars constant, the number of bars sold would increase. (This relationship between elasticity and revenue can be found in any introductory microeconomics text.) But if the demand for chocolate were inelastic, the number of bars sold would decrease.

Although it could be argued that the demand for any particular CD is elastic, since otherwise the seller would find it profitable to raise its price, it need not be the case that overall demand for CDs is elastic. CD prices are not set individually (see Silva and Ramello in note 25), and CDs would often seem to be close enough substitutes for each another that they could be classified in the same market (if you can't get a favorite group, you get another).

39. The area under these demands measures total value, and better sampling increases the total value for any given number of CDs purchased.

40. There were several other reports that were difficult to classify. Lawrence Lessig submitted a report that the court rejected out of hand, stating: "The Lessig Report merely offers a combination of legal opinion and editorial comment on Internet policy. Therefore, this Court grants plaintiffs' motion to exclude it."

41. The preliminary injunction preventing Napster from allowing users to download copyrighted files is in place, and Napster was effectively shut down in the form in which it previously existed. Napster is now planning to return as a legitimate subscription service.

42. The court told Napster to end the dissemination of copyrighted materials. Napster did this by blocking access to known copyrighted songs, which required many different variations for each title since users tried to evade being blocked by putting up alternative titles that still indicated what the song was. When Napster was only 99 percent effective in this endeavor, the judge threatened to shut it down.

43. These reports are so named in the "Memorandum and Order Re Admissibility of Expert Reports" issued by the trial judge. Plaintiffs also had a declaration by Charles Robbins, a store owner claiming that Napster had largely destroyed his business, but this report was thoroughly discredited by the Fader report (discussed in detail on pages 172–173), which pointed out that the store had changed locations

and switched from selling new CDs to selling used records and CDs during the period that its sales declined.

44. Actually, the Fine study looks at three groups of bricks-and-mortar retailers: the overall set, a set of retailers near the forty most heavily wired college campuses, and a set of retailers near college campuses that have banned Napster. Napster's expert Hall makes much of the fact that this latter group of retailers shows the same decrease in sales as the others, claiming that for this group, sales should improve if Napster were having a negative impact on sales. Such a claim is unwarranted since we do not know how long Napster had been banned on these campuses and how successful the ban was.

45. It is unfortunate that online CD retailers probably had not achieved an equilibrium market position prior to Napster's arrival on the scene because comparing the sales of online retailers to bricks-and-mortar retailers would have provided what would probably have been a better test of Napster's impact, with online sales changes being the proxy for Napster's impact.

46. Fine reports that online sales figures were first collected in the first quarter of 1999.

47. The court was also aware of these problems: "The Court finds some aspects of the Fine Report troubling—especially the fact that it shows a decline in retail sales prior to the launching of Napster. This limitation, combined with Fine's decision not to track Internet music sales, reduces the study's probative value."

48. Nevertheless, at its peak Napster downloads were estimated to be in the vicinity of 2.8 billion files per month, which would be roughly the equivalent of 250 million CDs per month. I suspect that these data include many failed downloads. According to the Fine report, U.S. national sales ran approximately 60 million CDs per month. So, even with the slow bandwidths, the potential impact was large. See "Music Downloads Soar" Reuters, September 6, 2001, available at *http://news.cnet.com/news/0-1005-200-7080479.html.*

49. Jay includes "getting free music" and "getting music that one wants" as other answers that reveal substitution of sales. Although this might be true, it is not clearly so, and this interpretation problem could have been avoided if more direct questions had been asked.

50. The court states (in the Memorandum and Order mentioned in footnote 43): "He considers himself an expert on consumer surveys. . . . However, he admitted in his deposition that he has never before prepared a consumer survey for litigation and he is unfamiliar with the standards set forth by federal courts for the reliability of such surveys." Lack of familiarity with legal standards hardly disqualifies someone as an authority on surveys in general. The court continues: "In short, his claim to have designed and overseen the Greenfield survey appears exaggerated, and the generality of his report renders it of dubious reliability and value."

51. Hall assumes that any music sampling by Napster users benefits the CD market, an assumption that we demonstrated to be incorrect in the subsection, Exposure Effects (p. 165).

52. The court stated: "Hall relied too heavily on outside studies that favored defendant without performing any analysis of the Jay Report . . . these shortcomings are not grave enough to warrant exclusion of his expert opinion. Insofar as the Hall Report assumes the requested injunction would put defendant out of business, it tends to corroborate plaintiffs' argument that Napster has no legitimate non-infringing uses . . . they [the plaintiffs] would be wise not to object too strenuously to admission of the Hall Report."

53. One potentially questionable point, according to Hall, is Teece's use of the concept of path dependence to argue that consumers will be locked in to Napster and will not then purchase music online from the copyright owners. Hall notes that Teece cites the QWERTY keyboard as an example of such lock-in. Readers who have made it this far will recognize my problems with this line of argument, particularly since Teece is keenly aware of the problems with the QWERTY story. Second, it is hard to imagine what the coordination problem might be that would have to underlie a case of lock-in since network

effects are not sufficient for there to be lock-in without some form of coordination failure. (Hall cites my 1990 article with Margolis in rebuttal to Teece.)

54. The judge's readings of the reports seem, to me, to have been biased against Napster even though I think her decision was in the end correct even if not supported by the evidence at hand.

55. This distinction is somewhat artificial. Napster is also a peer-to-peer system, albeit one with a central server. And the pure peer-to-peer-based systems can have some specialized hardware—LimeWire, for example, has a special router that is supposed to improve performance.

56. The claim is made that the four largest Napster replacements, Fast-Track, Audiogalaxy, iMesh, and Gnutella, were responsible for 3.05 billion downloaded files although not all of these were songs. The data comes from Webnoize, a company that tracks Internet usage as reported by Reuters as discussed in note 48.

57. See Lee Gomes, "Recording Industry Targets Gnutella Amid Signs Napster Usage Is Falling," *Wall Street Journal*, May 4, 2001, page B6.

58. For one of the more subdued articles on this issue see "Okay, Six Choruses of 'Kumbaya'—That'll Be $1.50" by Marcus Errico, *E! Online*, August 24, 1996, at *http://www.eonline.com/News/Items/ 0,1,109,00.html*. For ASCAP's version of this public relations fiasco see ASCAP's memo "ASCAP Clarifies Position on Music in Girl Scout Camps," August 26, 1996, at *http://www.ascap.com/press/ ascap-082696.html*.

59. For example, LimeWire has an "Anti-Freeloader Feature": In the FAQ (frequently asked questions) file for Limewire we find: "Q: Will the number of files I share affect my LimeWire experience? A: It could. If you're not sharing enough files, users with certain connection preferences won't let you connect to them for downloading. For this reason, we recommend all LimeWire users share generously with one another."

60. If Napster were to have a no-freeload rule, one might think that competition between Napster and a decentralized system would favor a decentralized system since freeloaders would flock there and almost everyone would want to be a freeloader. But such is not necessarily the case. The system with a no-freeload rule would have more heavily demanded files available for downloading relative to the number of downloaders and should therefore prove more attractive to users, particularly users with files to upload. What economists refer to as a separating equilibrium might come to exist, with Napster having the newer and still popular songs, whereas the pure peer-to-peer networks would have older songs.

61. One problem is that credit card companies currently charge a relatively large fixed fee for each transaction that tends to negate the usefulness of micropayments. This will presumably be fixed someday.

62. For example, to test the effectiveness of watermarks, a technology that in principle allows the tracking of the origin of a copy, the Secure Digital Music Initiative (SDMI) last year sponsored a hacking challenge, offering $10,000 to anyone who could successfully remove the watermarks while meeting certain audio-quality standards. That challenge was met, and a minor brouhaha took place over whether the codebreakers (a group from Princeton) were to be allowed to publish their techniques, which they eventually did. See "SDMI hack draws legal threats," Lisa M. Bowman, *ZDNet News,* April 23, 2001, found here *http://www.zdnet.com/zdnn/stories/ news/0,4586,5081595,00.html.* The report of the hackers can be found at *http://www.theregister.co.uk/extra/sdmi-attack.htm.*

63. Of course, digital copies can be used to make another generation of digital copies that are of the same quality, whereas analog copies of copies deteriorate in quality for each additional generation.

64. See Pamela Samuelson "The Copyright Grab," *Wired,* January 1996, found here: *http://www.wired.com/wired/archive/4.01/white.paper_ pr.html.*

65. Lessig states: "Code displaces the balance in copyright law and doctrines such as fair use." Lawrence Lessig, *Code and Other Laws of Cyberspace*, (New York, Basic Books, 1999), p. 135.

66. Bell points out that fair use imposes costs of its own on the copier (copying costs such as photocopiers, time, etc.) and also imposes uncertainty on users since it is often unclear whether individual acts are fair use or not. He also moves a bit in the direction of the efficiency of perfect price discrimination that I put forth when he suggests that many instances of worthwhile copying would be missed because getting permission was too costly, but that DRM reduces these transactions, potentially increasing the number of such uses. See Tom W. Bell, "Fair Use vs. Fared Use: The Impact of Automated Rights Management on Copyright's Fair Use Doctrine" *North Carolina Law Review*, vol. 76, (1998): 558–618. Available at *http://www.tomwbell.com/writings/FullFared.html*

67. "Economists have long understood that granting property rights over information is dangerous (to say the least). This is not because of leftist leanings among economists. It is because economists are pragmatists, and their objective in granting any property right is simply to facilitate production, but there is no way to know, in principle, whether increasing or decreasing the rights granted under intellectual property law will lead to an increase in the production of an intellectual property." Lessig, *Code and Other Laws of Cyberspace*, p. 134.

68. Wendy Gordon, "Fair Use as Market Failure: A Structural and Economic Analysis of the Betamax Case and Its Predecessors," *Columbia Law Review*, vol. 82, pp. 1600–1657.

69. I assume that the more one uses of a product, the greater one's willingness to pay.

70. The harm from the reduced output is traditionally referred to as a deadweight or welfare loss in economics textbooks.

71. W. M. Landes and R. A. Posner, "An Economic Analysis of Copyright Law," *Journal of Legal Studies* 18, no. 2 (June 1989): 325–363. One

might argue that earlier, Plant (1934), referenced in note 4, also thought that lengthening copyright would not increase production since he argued that copyright wasn't even necessary. This is, I believe, a misreading of his work. Plant doesn't argue that production is generally unaffected by income although he does point out that this is true for some authors. Instead he argues primarily that the profits from being first to market (prior to 1934, when copying was still slow and costly) were great enough that authors received all of the reward they needed.

72. Unlike patent law, copyright does not prevent others from creating the same expression of an idea as long as the later expressions were independently created. So, if you can prove that a sonnet you wrote, which happens to be identical to one written by Shakespeare, was created entirely on your own, it will not be a copyright infringement. In patent law, even if later inventors were entirely independent in creating their invention, if it is turns out to be similar to the first patent, it will not be allowed to stand as an independent patent. This can be contrasted with trademarked characters, which cannot be copied. So, although there may be fewer stories with Mickey Mouse in them, the profits generated by Disney's rodent provide incentives for others to create their own animal icons.

73. It can be claimed that the DRM might impose a contract on the user that no copies of any sort are to be made as a condition of sale. But any book, even with no digital technology at all, could come shrink wrapped with a contract that says to only open it if you promise not to make copies. That is the nature of many software contracts. So this problem really has little to do with DRM.

74. See page 591 of Bell, referenced in note 66, where he discusses the legal impacts of DRM on cutting and pasting.

75. It has been suggested by Neil Weinstock Netanel ("Copyright and a Democratic Civil Society," *Yale Law Journal* 106 (1996): 283–386) that fair use is valuable to society even if perfect metering reduced transaction costs to zero because, in his view, the purpose of copy-

right is to promote a democratic society and not to maximize economic efficiency. He believes that fair use protects negative follow-up works, i.e., parodies, that he suggests could be eliminated by the original copyright owner with strong enough copyright protection. This, to me, confuses censorship with the proper working of markets.

76. See Declan McCullagh, "New Copyright Bill Heading to DC," *Wired News,* September 7, 2001, available at *http://www.wired.com/news/ politics/0,1283,46655,00.html.*

77. The two leading services that have been announced, MusicNet (supported by Warner, Bertelsmann, and EMI) and Pressplay (supported by Sony and Vivendi) have suggested some form of monthly subscription fee. The suggestions, however, are for a fixed number of downloads. Reports *Newsbytes*: "[A]cting MusicNet CEO Rob Glaser said the lower end of a hypothetical tiered pricing plan might include a $9.95 per month plan allowing customers to temporarily download 30 songs and stream 30 titles." That same article reports on a survey on teenage users indicating they would be willing to pay slightly under $3 per month for unlimited downloads. See Brian Krebs, "Plug.In: Music Services May Struggle With Napster-Era Teens," *Newsbytes,* July 26, 2001 at *http://www.newsbytes.com/news/01/ 168370.html.*

   A more recent article discusses the problems with selling music online, particularly since these sites intend to stream music, which brings in performing rights as well as other rights. See Jim Hu and John Borland, "Label Deal to Unclog Music Logjam" *Cnet News,* September 17, 2001, available at *http://www.msnbc.com/news/630261. asp?0na=22184D02.*

78. On December 19, 2001, Pressplay officially announced its pricing: Ten dollars per month for 30 downloads plus 300 streams (listening to a song) at the low end. Twenty-five dollars per month for 100 downloads, 1,000 streams, and 20 burns (songs put on a CD). There is also a monthly limit of two burns per month per artist. The limit

of two burns per month will tend to keep the service from being a substitute for album sales.

79. For a copy of the act, which does contain some useful provisions, see *http://www.house.gov/boucher/moca-page.htm.*

80. The analysis tends to go the other way. Separate wholesale and retail channels, if they are not perfectly competitive, both tend to put their own supercompetitive markups on the product, causing more harm than would be the case for a single integrated channel, a result known as double marginalization.

Chapter 8

Conclusion

Whither Supply and Demand?

On January 3, 2000, the first work day of a new millennium, the *Wall Street Journal* published an entire multipage section of the newspaper that should soon be a collector's item.[1] The articles in that section nicely embodied many of the ideas that I have discussed in the preceding pages. Ironically, most of the claims that were made in these articles were only months away from being unraveled by the events that were soon to unfold. One of the more amusing articles was titled "So Long Supply and Demand."[2]

The supposed death of supply and demand was born of monumental hubris championed most fervently by those largely unschooled in economic analysis. For example, the author of that article provided several illustrations of how this belief had entered managerial thinking. He quoted Mark McElroy, a principal in International Business Machines Corporation's Global Knowledge Management Practice, as saying, "Conventional economics is dead. Deal with it!" He also quoted Danny Hillis, vice president of research and development at the Walt Disney Company, as saying that the new economy "is actually much broader than technology alone. It is a new way of thinking."

Thomas Petzinger, the author of that article, and my foil for the next few pages, explains that mainstream economists were loath to accept the fact that their prized theories were no longer applicable in the new economy:

206

You can understand why economists throw cold water on the new-economy concept, since accepting it would require them to abandon many of their dearest tools and techniques. It has become clichéd to cite the historian Thomas Kuhn's 40-year-old concept of a "paradigm shift"—a revolution in knowledge that forces scientists to give up the beliefs on which they have staked their careers. But that's exactly what economics and accountants could be facing.

It is instructive to follow Petzinger in his thinking since it nicely encapsulates many of the points that were made in previous chapters. What was it that was causing the concepts of supply and demand to be overturned? He provides several reasons.

First, he claims, the sources of wealth had changed.

On an economywide level, these accelerating improvements may now be entering a supercritical phase in which they compound exponentially. Inventories, which once triggered or prolonged recessions, are not just declining but in many places evaporating . . . "Economists fail to realize that these improvements are reducing costs so radically as to enable entirely new ways of doing business," says telecom consultant David Isenberg of isen.com, Westfield, N.J. . . . Creativity is overtaking capital as the principal elixir of growth. And creativity, although precious, shares few of the constraints that limit the range and availability of capital and physical goods. "In a knowledge-based economy, there are no constraints to growth," says Michael Mauboussin, CS First Boston's managing director of equity research. "Man alive! That's not something new?"

It should be easy to recognize that almost all of the ideas in this paragraph are complete nonsense. (If not, go back and read the earlier chapters!) But for many industry analysts prior to the Internet meltdown, these claims seemed perfectly reasonable, and anyone who didn't believe them just "didn't get it."[3] Economists were often accused of just that, in part because the basic premise of economics has always been that scarcity is an unfortunate fact of life, Internet or no Internet. This scarcity assumption, although a bit of a downer, is not going to be overturned. Beware anyone who says otherwise. Note, however, that some of the claimed new ideas in the above paragraph were not even new. For example, economists have long known that capital is *not* the major ingredient in growth and that new knowledge *is* the most important factor in economic growth.

The second major reason that the old economics failed, according to Petzinger, was that the fundamentals of pricing and distribution had changed. Here his arguments should have a very familiar ring, and some of our old friends reappear as authorities supporting this view.

> In his classic undergraduate text *Economics*, Paul Samuelson noted that any second grader could figure out that increased supplies cause lower value. But that was before Windows 95, automatic teller machines, and Nike shoes. Products used in networks—whether computing, financial, or social—increase in unit value as the supply increases . . . Former Stanford economist W. Brian Arthur has popularized this more-begets-more concept under the banner of "increasing returns." The timeless notion of diminishing returns isn't dead, of course, but it applies to an ever-shrinking proportion of value-added activity, such as grain harvests and polyvinyl-chloride production. . . . This explains why a seemingly insane strategy such as giving away your basic product has become a strategy of choice in the new economy. . . . [T]he vendor collects revenue from another source, such as from selling upgrades, support, or advertising. (Radio and television broadcasters—

networks, after all—have always operated this way.)
Another network, the cell-phone system, exploded when
telecom companies began providing phones for practically
nothing, even free of charge, and reaping increasing returns from air-time charges. . . .

The future for economists surely looked bleak to Mr. Petzinger. Economists are relegated to studying those few markets
like "grain harvests and polyvinyl-chloride production"—
whatever those two markets might have in common. Note that
Mr. Petzinger apparently makes the fundamental error of assuming that television networks have network effects just because
they called themselves networks. He also believed, incorrectly,
that network effects somehow naturally led to advertising-based
revenue models, apparently as a result of the facile comparison of
television "networks" with the Internet "network." His claim that
cell-phone systems reap increasing returns from air-time charges
revealed a lack of understanding of that concept as well.
He continues:

Our 500-year-old system of accounting has grave limitations in this world. But for now, according to the CS First
Boston atoms-to-bits report, "there is a substantial and
growing chasm between our accounting system and economic reality" . . . [I]n an economy awash in capital, the
endgame, not the score at the end of each quarter, is all
that counts. . . . "Earnings are a decision variable, not a
requirement," says Prof. Arthur, the economist. "If everyone thinks you're doing fine without earnings, why have
them?"

This is a truly amazing quote. Why have earnings? Do we
really need to ask? What, after all, is the value of a piece of stock
if the underlying company doesn't have any earnings to show?

Surely Professor Arthur has been misquoted. Or then again, maybe not.

And since traditional accounting practices didn't seem to agree that money-losing practices were the road to riches, they were to be thrown out along with all those other outdated ideas that economists were fond of. Except, of course, for Professor Arthur's ideas.[4] Apparently, a little knowledge can be a dangerous thing, but a little mis-knowledge can be even more dangerous.

Finally, Mr. Petzinger thinks that the structure of economic decision-making had changed.

> Knowledge-fueled growth and hyperefficiency account for only part of the this robustness. One additional factor is that the economy is smarter than ever . . . "At one time, if you had 50 or 100 giant companies doing the same thing in lockstep at the same time, you could destroy an economy," says Mr. Birch of Cognetics. "But you don't have that anymore."

When words like "hyper" start appearing as prefixes in paragraphs that have nothing to do with mathematics, it is usually a sign to start looking for a shovel. But in an odd way, the point Mr. Birch makes is valid, although not in the specifics he gives. Mr. Birch was wrong about which firms were marching in lockstep. The firms marching in lockstep were the Internet firms, and the old-fashioned firms, the ones that didn't follow the advice to "get it," are the ones who didn't march. As it is, a large enough number of firms (usually start-ups) did march, like lemmings in lockstep, right off the cliff. If the entire economy had gone the way of the Internet firms, we would be in pretty big trouble. The dinosaurs, in other words, saved the economy from a far worse fate.

Lessons

Making fun of the poorly thought-out ideas that were so common just a year or two ago is great sport, but it hides a more serious agenda. The general rules that have formed our understanding of markets have been developed over a period of centuries. Every now and then a new "paradigm" is presented as a replacement. The death of supply and demand has been prematurely announced numerous times. But, like a modern horror-movie villain, supply and demand keep rising from the grave. They do so because they provide a wonderful tool that imparts extremely useful knowledge about markets.

The most recent new paradigm is the Internet economy, which was supposed to stand the old rules about markets and economies on their collective heads. The laws of supply and demand are not so fragile as to be overcome by anything so small as a new method of communicating with each another. After all, economic laws have survived the invention of the steam engine, the harnessing of electricity, the invention of the telephone, the radio, the television, and the computer, as well as the atom bomb. Long after the Internet craze is an interesting footnote in history, the rules of supply and demand will continue to describe the behavior of markets.

I do not want to diminish the fact that life changes—and technology along with it. That sometimes there is something new under the sun. That often, our theories and ideas turn out to be wrong. But the new theories and ideas that have been put forward in this instance are not more powerful alternatives that tell us something new and truthful about the world. Sometimes— probably more often than not—the new and intriguing ideas turn out to be wrong ideas. In this case, the new ideas had largely been demonstrated to be wrong before the Internet craze took off. But only a handful of academics were aware of these events. And truth is often less important than glamour.

A facile reading of the previous chapters might give the impression that there really is nothing new or different about conducting business on the Internet. That is not quite accurate.

Because the Internet enhances the transmission of information, the role of information is enhanced. Information, as a product, has some characteristics that are very different from those of more traditional products.

The previous chapters provide a set of rules for the reader wondering how to use the Internet to best advantage. They warn against the expectations of quick and easy riches, of rushing off to catch the wave, of eschewing product quality because of the delay it might cause to product introduction. They reaffirm old standards such as "Slow and steady wins the race," "Build a better mousetrap," and "There's a sucker born every minute."

Readers should understand that business on the Internet is likely to be at least as competitive as business in the bricks-and-mortar world. There will be no easy cornucopia of profits. Instead, companies will need to create superior and difficult-to-imitate business models. They will have to discover the products that work best when sold over the Internet. They will have to figure out efficient pricing mechanisms. They will have to refrain from wasting vast resources in a mad race to be first in a market because being first is not the key to long-term success.

Most important, I hope these chapters provide some understanding and, hopefully, appreciation of how markets work, both the high-tech variety and the more traditional kind. Readers will understand how it is that markets generate profits, and they will hopefully learn that you can't correctly analyze a market by looking only at demand or only at supply. And that you certainly cannot correctly understand a market by ignoring both.

If you understand this, you understand most of what you need to know about Internet markets and, to a large extent, you understand what you need to know about most other markets. That is the most important lesson that was lost in the last few years.

Notes

1. Apologies to millennium purists such as my daughter Lauren, who will point out that the new millennium began in the year 2001.

2. Thomas Petzinger Jr., "So Long, Supply and Demand: There's a New Economy Out There—And It Looks Nothing Like the Old One," *Wall Street Journal,* January 3, 2000, page S1.

3. At the risk of being labeled change-impaired by the change-management gurus, it is fair to say that most of what are labeled as new ways of thinking are mostly just wrong ways of thinking. The few new thoughts that turn out to be better than the old will, in due course, become part of the received wisdom with which later "new" ideas will do battle.

4. At the risk of appearing snide, my understanding is that Professor Arthur doesn't really have a doctorate in economics, but instead has one in operations research. On the other hand, he did publish articles in economics journals and does have a following within the field.

Index